Child's Play

an activities and materials handbook

Barbara R. Trencher

Humanics Limited
Atlanta, Georgia

Humanics Limited
P.O. Box 7447
Atlanta, Georgia 30309

On the cover: The design on the crayons represents a trademark of Crayola.

Third Printing 1991

PRINTED IN THE UNITED STATES OF AMERICA

ISBN 0-89334-003-0

contents

Dedication . . . . *i*

Acknowledgements . . . . *i*

Introduction . . . . *vii*

part 1 space planning and design

Introduction 1
Designing Indoor and Outdoor Space 2
Characteristics of Well Defined Spaces 3
    Activity Centers 6
The Quadrant Approach 8
Floor Plans 9
General Classroom Arrangement Checklist 10
Selected References 14

part 2 awareness of the arts

Introduction 17
Art Questionaire 19
Brush Painting 20
Finger Painting 21
    Related Color Activities 23
Modeling 24
    Clay 24
    Playdough 26
    Sawdust Molding 26
    Paper Mache 28
Collage 29
Construction and Mobiles 30
Tearing, Cutting and Pasting 31
Printing 32
    Vegetable Printing 32
    Glass Printing 32
    Linoleum Block Printing 33
Color Media 34
    Colored Chalk 34
    Craypas 34
    Crayons 34
Puppets 35
    Puppet Theatres 36
Selected References 37

part 3 the song is love

Introduction 39
Experiences with Movement 40
    Exercises with Instruments 43
    Experiences with Chants, Finger Plays and Poems . . 44
    Rhythmic Chants 44
    Finger Plays 46
    Familiar Children's Poems 47
Easily Constructed Musical Instruments 52
Selected References 55

part 4 one two buckle my shoe

Introduction 57
One to One Correspondence 58
    Puzzle Cards 58
    Dominoes 60
    String Board 60
    Pick Up Sticks 61
Numerals 62
    Number Songs and Finger Plays 63
Sets and Classification 65
    Attribute Cards 65
    Set Lotto 66
    Classification 66
    Sorting, Grouping and Classifying 67
Geometric Shapes and Their Relationships 68
    Cardboard Squares 68
    Geoboards 68
    Tangram 69
    Block Building 72
Ordering 73
    Copying Patterns 73
Measuring 75
    Graphing 75
    Scales 76
    Water Play 77
Selected References 79

part 5 a time for words

Introduction 81
Speaking 83
    V.I.P. Bulletin Board 83
    Body Tracing 83
    Classroom Picture Wheel 84
    Literature 84
    Spoken Poetry – Choral Speaking 84
    Story Telling and Dramatic Play 86
    Language Experiences with Blocks 87

Listening 88
    Poetry 89
    Games that Aid in the Development of Listening Skills 89
    Tape Recording 90
Reading 90
    The Basal Approach 90
    Total Communication (Language Experience) 91
    Individualized Reading 91
    Independent Reading 91
    Symbols 91
    Word Picture Dominoes 92
Writing 92
    Individual Dictionaries 92
    Words as Pictures 92
    Name and Word Recognition 93
    Learning Letter Names 93
    Wheel of Fortune 93
    Book Binding 94
Discrimination and Recognition 95
    Auditory Discrimination 95
    Auditory Recognition 95
    Letter Discrimination 95
    Visual Recognition 96
Selected References

part 6 ask the wizard

Introduction 101
The Senses 103
    Sight 103
    Smell 104
    Touch 105
    Taste 106
    Sound 107
Electricity 109
    Electric Charges 109
    Current Electricity 109
    Experiments with Electricity 110
Magnetism 110
    What Do Magnets Attract? 110
    Magnets Have Poles 110
    Electromagnets 111
Living Things 111
    Fall Planting. 112
    Fall Art Projects 112
    Terrarium. 112
    Spring and Summer Planting 113
    Spring Activities 114
    Winter Weather. 114

Measurement and Volume 116
    Measuring Volume 116
    Floating and Sinking 116
    Dry Sand 116
Selected References 119

part 7   child's play cook book

Introduction 121
    No Access to a Kitchen 122
    No Available Stove 122
    No Budget for Cooking 122
    Safety in Cooking 123
    Preparing Experience Charts 124
    Preparation of Stone Soup 125
    How Many Should Cook 126
Breakfast and Healthy Baked Snacks 127
General Snacks 131
Fruit and Vegetable Treats 133
Party and Holiday Favorites 137
Selected References 145

APPENDIX

Developmental Guidelines 146

Selected References 156

Introduction

"A child said, 'What is the grass?' fetching it to me with full hands. How could I answer the child? I do not know what it is any more than he . . .

Walt Whitman
Song of Myself

This book is not a curriculum guide in the traditional sense of the word. Creative people who work with children usually stuff curriculum guides into their drawers or press leaves in them which are collected on their latest nature walks. This is also not a "how to do it book" which tells you the only way to teach the numeral 10 at 9:30 on Monday morning. Finally, this book is not a version of Websters Unabridged Dictionary including everything that has been written about what to do with preschool children.

Child's Play is a humanistic approach to the presentation of activities and materials used with preschool children. Its goal is the establishment of positive experiences and sound inter-

Whitman, Walt, "Song of Myself", *Leaves of Grass.* New York: Doubleday and Co., 1940, p. 39.

personal relationships between adults and children, which focus on the process rather than the product of learning. As an eclectic combination of activities gathered from parents and teachers of preschool children, *Child's Play* has proven helpful in guiding preschool children through their active days.

To be used effectively, *Child's Play* should become personal for each person who uses it. You, the readers, are encouraged to use it as a workbook, writing in its large margins and contributing new ideas. Only you can make the experiences on its pages come alive. Your efforts will combine with the children's to facilitate social-emotional, and intellectual growth.

THIS BOOK BELONGS TO:

part 1 / space planning and design

Introduction
Designing Indoor and Outdoor Space
Characteristics of Well Designed Spaces
A Quadrant Approach to Classroom Design
Floor Plans
General Classroom Arrangement Checklist
Selected References

Introduction

School, to have the maximum effect, should not be an island, but part of a physical context conceived as a function of the requirements of education. It should not be a closed apparatus but a structure spread out of a network of social activities capable of articulating itself by its contextual variations.

Giancarlo De Carlo

Young children are naturally curious, active and inventive, especially when placed in environments which are flexible and interesting. Their behavior is influenced by the arrangement of physical space and the selection of materials in their classroom (Shure, 1963, Kritchevsky, 1969, Prescott, Kritchevsky and Jones, 1972.) There is also a relationship between the interactions which take place between children and adults and the specific activities which occur at different times during the day. For example, one would expect conversation during a morning art project to be related to that project, while conversation during lunch to be less concerned with art, although the same table is used for both activities.

DeCarlo, Giancarlo. *Why and How to Build School Buildings,* Harvard Educational Review, Vol. XXXIX, No. 4, 1969, p. 22.

1

A flexible environment for young children is one in which organized space facilitates free exploration of material, use of imagination and working at one's own pace. An old trunk for example, may be used as a treasure chest, or a space ship, or a lemonade stand depending on teacher and children's imagination. Simple materials become multi-purpose aids and useful props for stimulating the creative activities of children.

Poor organization of space can inhibit the physical, social and intellectual development of children. It is characterized by dead, uninteresting and unusable space. Poor organization of space contributes to social conflict, confusion over program goals, congestion, loss of attention and ultimately, loss of freedom for both adults and children.

Designing Indoor and Outdoor Space

Designing indoor and outdoor space begins with the consideration of four kinds of physical space defined by school architect William Caudill (1968):

Expansible space —
    space which allows for ordered growth.
Versatile space —
    space which serves many functions at the same time.
Convertible space —
    space which is economically adapted to program changes.
Malleable space —
    space which can be changed at will and at once.

Designing indoor and outdoor play spaces also includes considerations of the characteristics of color, lighting and texture. Well designed spaces for young children have the same characteristics as comfortable lived in homes. Children respond positively to warm colors of red, yellow and orange, as well as the cool hues of blue and green. Paintings and photographs placed at the child's eye level enhance the learning environment as they would at home. Lighting and temperature considerations include natural as well as varied artificially controlled conditions which are easily manipulated by children as well as adults. Finally, a variety of textures on floor, walls and ceiling contributes to the aesthetic and practical use of early childhood facilities.

Educational Facilities Laboratory. *Educational Change and Architectural Consequences: A Report on Facilities for Individualized Instruction.* N. Y., N. Y.: 1968, p. 15.

Characteristics of
Well Defined Spaces

Planned indoor and outdoor spaces are an integral part of a child's learning environment and as such provide additional opportunities for physical and social development, exploration and curiosity. Equally important are additional outdoor facilities such as parks, woods, city streets and shopping areas which provide opportunities for further exploration. School environments which are well designed help children learn more about themselves and their world. These environments include the following:

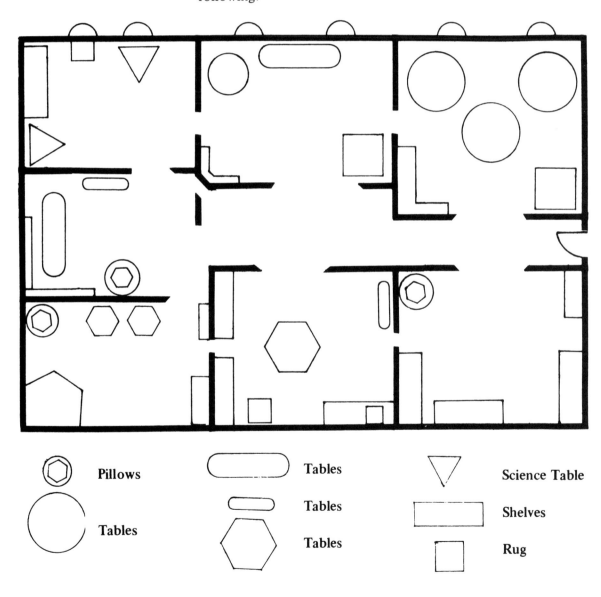

⬡ Pillows	▭ Tables	▽ Science Table
◯ Tables	▭ Tables	▭ Shelves
	⬡ Tables	▢ Rug

— Well designed pathways and empty floor spaces. These allow children and adults to move comfortably from one area to another. Well designed paths function as well defined highways, providing easy access to each play area.

— Separate non-conflicting work areas. These areas are designed to separate wet and dry activities, quiet and noisy activities, and activities for large and small muscles development as well as providing protection to children and materials.

—Distinctly divided and organized areas. These areas provide a sense of order by insuring a proper place for each material to be stored for adults as well as children. Organized areas reflect order and relate directly to activities going on in and out of doors. Areas can be organized by providing multi-sized containers to facilitate the proper sorting of material. Organization is also aided by properly labeling the shelves.

— Appropriate child and adult storage areas. These are needed if children are to develop a respect for individual property. They provide carefully planned spaces in and out of children's reach. Appropriately planned adult storage spaces eliminate the need for negative comments such as: "Don't use the stapler. It's for the teacher." At the same time, low, open well-equipped shelves aid in children's independent selection of materials and minimize the need for constant adult supervision.

—Private areas. These areas are ideally ones into which adults cannot comfortably fit. They indicate an adult's recognition and respect for children's need to be alone at times during the day. Small window seats, caves, cubby holes, small structures which are boxed off, provide this atmosphere.

—Active areas. Both indoor and outdoor space should include areas and facilities for climbing, jumping, swinging, tumbling and crawling.

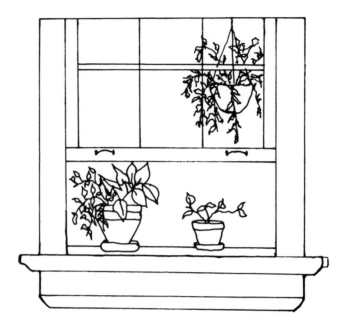

— Areas for living things. Areas for plants and animals do not need to be placed together but can be scattered in and out of doors. They provide natural additions to the environment as well as offering a means of teaching responsibility and care of living things.

ACTIVITY CENTERS

Well stocked art areas for collage, paste, scissors, brushes, magazines, newspapers, three-dimensional art materials, recycled art material.

House, store, office and mystery area large enough for dramatic and fantasy play appropriate for boys and girls.

Sand and water play area, including a workbench which is protected to minimize the potential danger to passing children, yet is within easy access for an adult.

Library corner including restful private spaces for thinking and relaxing.

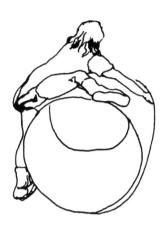

Science area complete with tinkering and junk material to take apart, magnets, batteries, growing plants, fossils.

Manipulative toys and table games in a multi-purpose space that may be planned on more than one level to accommodate small·groups of children.

A large protected space away from traffic for blocks. Different sized blocks, hollow, unit, and cardboard serve different building needs and therefore do not necessarily have to be placed together.

Large area both in and out of doors for large-muscle activity to include play frames for climbing, tumbling mat, boards, slides and tubes.

Multi-purpose open space for movement, dance group meetings, plays, stories, snack and lunch. This space can also be used for napping.

The Quadrant Approach

**This is one way to approach classroom design.
Is it appropriate for you?**

Dry

Quiet — Noisey

Wet

Writing
Listening Center
Puzzles
Math Area
Drawing

Blocks
Manipulative Toys
Clay, Puzzles
Drama, Movement
Wood Working

Collage
Pasting
Finger Painting
Easel Painting

Clay
Cooking
Water Play

Floor Plans

Here are three other simple drawings.
Can you find?

The Dead Space
The Private Space
The Paths
The Incompatible Areas.

Do you like any of these designs?
How would you improve them if you could?

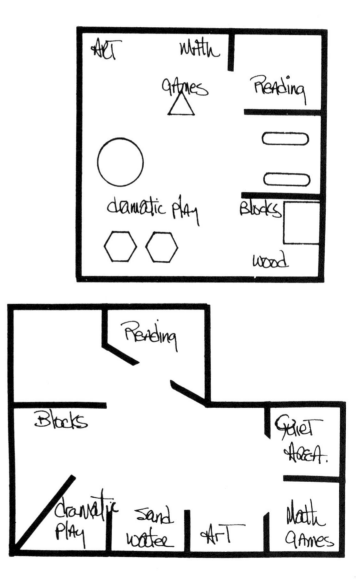

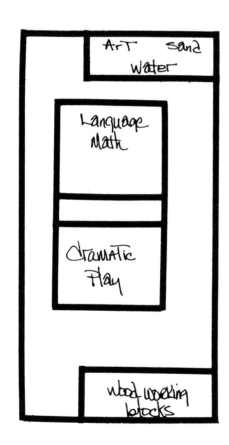

General Classroom Arrangement Checklist

This is an inventory of physical space in a preschool classroom. Check the characteristics which appropriately apply to your room. Do you want to make any changes?

PRESCHOOL ROOM*

Physical Arrangement

____ the room is arranged in distinct learning areas or interest centers

____ the room is an open space without distinct learning areas

____ there are some learning areas but the room is mostly open space

____ different rooms contain different learning areas

____ one room contains all learning areas

____ the room is divided by partitions, describe (include height)

____ the room has no partitions and is a large room

____ furniture arrangement eliminates or encloses wide open space and serves to prevent distraction and disruptive running

____ the room has no partitions and is a small room

____ partitions are adjustable (flexible) to adapt to different activities

____ partitions are fixed and cannot be easily rearranged with adaptability

____ furniture is moveable to permit rearranging for differing activities (nap, groups, etc.)

____ furniture is fixed and not easily adjusted

____ adjacent learning areas are compatible and do not distract neighboring activities

____ adjacent learning areas cause distraction

____ there are quiet and private areas removed from classroom activities

____ quiet and private areas exist but are not protected from classroom activities

____ there are no designated quiet or private areas

*Designed by Annette Sheehan, Doctoral Student, Georgia State University, Department of Early Childhood Education

___ one table or more is separated for individual solitary work without distraction

___ the following maintenance facilities are easily available for the child:

___ cubbies
___ coat hooks
___ toilets
___ water for drinking
___ water for washing up
___ housekeeping equipment
___ cots or sleeping facilities

___ the following furniture is child size:

___ chairs
___ tables
___ shelves
___ other _____

___ there is no table, or space which provides undistracted individual work

___ the following maintenance facilities require teacher's assistance:

___ cubbies
___ coat hooks
___ toilets
___ water for drinking
___ water for washing up
___ housekeeping equipment
___ cots or sleeping facilities

___ the following furniture is not child size:

___ chairs
___ tables
___ shelves
___ other _____

Comments: _____

_____

Materials

___ materials are displayed in orderly and visible manner (not stacked 3 or 4 items high and not placed one in front of another on a deep shelf)

___ materials are stacked 3 or 4 items high and/or one in front of the other.

___ spaces for materials are well defined (i.e. – with labels, sorting containers, color coding)

___ once the material is removed from its place the child must rely on memory when returning it to its place

___ materials are located on child height shelves and can be obtained without teacher assistance

___ material must be transported to another part of the room for space to work

___ materials not to be used by children, at this time, are stored out of view of the children

___ materials not to be used by children, are not stored out of view of the children

___ stored materials are neatly arranged

___ stored materials are disorganized

___ stored materials are accessible to teachers

___ stored materials are not accessible to teachers

Comments: _____

_____

Heat

___ the heat is adequate and comfortably warm in all areas

___ the room is too cold

___ the room is too warm

___ the temperature varies in different parts of the room

Comments: _____

_____

Child's Play: An Activities and Materials Handbook

Color

___ colors are pleasing and varied

___ colors are drab and dull

___ colors are too bright and over-
stimulating and do not match

Comments: _____

_____

Lighting

___ the lighting is good in all areas

___ the lighting is poor in some areas

___ the lighting can be controlled or
varied in some areas

___ the lighting is fixed and uncontrollable
in different areas

___ natural lighting (window) is used
when and where possible

___ natural lighting is never used

Comments: _____

_____

Texture

Describe the atmosphere of the room in a few words (regarding neatness, clutter, order, chaotic, pur-
poseful clutter, random clutter, full, empty, etc.)

___ there are hard, smooth areas for water play, painting, etc.

___ there are soft, comfortable areas with:

___ carpeting
___ mattresses
___ pillows
___ cushioned chairs

Comments: _____

_____

DESIGN YOUR IDEAL CLASSROOM IN THIS SPACE.

Selected References

Abramson, Paul. *Schools for Early Childhood Education.* New York: Educational Facilities Laboratory, 1970.

Allen, Lady of Hartwood, et. al., editors. *Space for Play: The Youngest Children.* Copenhagen: World Organization for Early Childhood Education, 1964.

Ackerman, James. Listening to Architecture. *Harvard Educational Review,* Volume XXXIX, No. 4, 1969, 3-11.

Ashley, Warren. Six Reasons to Reconsider Recycling Before Considering New Construction. *School Management,* Volume 17, No. 7, August, September, 1973, 17.

Bergquist, R. E., editor. *The Bing Nursery School, A Child's View.* Stanford, California: Stanford University, 1966. (ERIC Document Reproduction Service No. ED 036-975)

Caldwell, Bettye. What is the Optimal Learning Environment for the Young Child? In Joe L. Frost, *Early Childhood Education Rediscovered.* New York: Holt, Rinehart and Winston Inc., 1968.

Coles, Robert. Those Things They Call Schools. *Harvard Educational Review,* Vol. XXXIX, No. 4, 1969, 45-67.

Day, David, Sheehan, Robert. Elements of a Better Preschool. *Young Children,* Vol. XXX, No. 1, November, 1974, 15-23.

DeCarlo, Giancarlo. Why and How to Build School Buildings. *Harvard Educational Review,* Vol. XXXIX, No. 4, 1969, 12-34.

Educational Facilities Laboratory. *Educational Change and Architectural Consequences: A Report on Facilities for Individualized Instruction.* N. Y., N. Y.: author, 1968.

Educational Facilities Laboratory. *Found Spaces and Equipment for Children's Centers.* New York: Author, 1972.

Engel, Brenda. *The Informal Classroom.* Newton, Massachusetts: Educational Development Corporation, 1973.

Fleischman, Richard. What Should a Schoolhouse Look Like. *American School and University,* Vol. 46, No. 3, November, 1973, 22,24,26.

Gesell, A., Ilg, F.L., Ames, L. B., Rodell, J. L. *Infant and Child in the Culture of Today (* Rev. ed.). New York: Harper and Row, 1974.

Hertzberger, Herman. Montessori Primary School in Delft Holland. *Harvard Educational Review,* Vol. XXXIX, No. 4, 1969, 58-67.

Hill, Polly. Children and Space. *Habitat,* Vol. 7, No. 6, 1969, 19-23.

Innes, Robert, Environmental Forces in Open and Closed Classroom Settings. *Journal of Experimental Education,* Vol. 44, No. 4, Summer, 1973.

Kohn, Sherwood. *The Early Learning Center. Profiles of Significant Schools.* New York: Educational Facilities Laboratory, 1971.

Kritchevsky, Sybil, Prescott, Elizabeth, Walling, Lee. *Planning Physical Environments for Young Children.* Washington, D.C.: National Association for the Education of Young Children, 1969.

Johnson, M.W. The Effect on Behavior of Variation in Amount of Play Equipment. *Child Development,* Vol. VI, 1935a, 56-58.

Osmon, F. L. *Patterns for Designing Children's Centers.* New York: Educational Facilities Laboratory, 1971.

Peterson, George, Bishop, Robert, Michaels, Richard, Rath, Gustave. Children's Choice of Playground Equipment. *Journal of Applied Psychology,* Vol. 58, No. 2, 1973, 233-238.

Prangnell, Peter. The Friendly Object. *Harvard Educational Review,* Vol. XXXIX, No. 4, 1969, 36-41.

Prescott, Elizabeth, Kritchevsky, Sybil, Jones, Elizabeth. *Day Care as a Child Rearing Environment.* Washington, D.C.: National Association for the Education of Young Children, 1972.

Schlesinger, Joy. *Leicestershire Report – The Classroom Environment.* Washington, D.C.: H.E.W. Report. 1966 (ERIC Document Reproduction Service No. ED 027 964).

Shure, Myrna Beth. The Psychological Ecology of a Nursery School. *Child Development,* Vol. 34, 1963, 979-992.

Sunderlin, Sylvia (Assoc. Ed.). *Housing for Early Childhood Education.* Washington: Association for Childhood Education International, 1968.

Tanzman, Jack. The Guy Who Makes Your Building Work. *School Management,* Vol. 17, No. 7, September, 1973, 36,37,51.

Walz, Thomas, Willenbring, Georgianna, deMoll, Lane. Environmental Design. *Social Work Journal,* January, 1974, 38-46.

part 2 / awareness of the arts

Introduction
Art Questionaire
Brush Painting
Finger Painting
Modeling
Collage
Constructions and Mobiles
Tearing, Cutting and Pasting
Printing
Color Media
Puppets
Selected References

Introduction

Because every creative process involves the whole child and not only a segment of him, art education may well become the catalyst for a child centered education in which the individual and his creative potential are placed above the subject matter: in which his inner equilibrium may be considered as important as his scientific achievements."

Viktor Lowenfeld

Viktor Lowenfeld made this statement in 1957 expressing a belief that development of the individual is the most powerful influence in education to date. The creative learning process is involved in every aspect of activities for children. According to Lowenfeld, introduction of art into the curriculum may well mean the difference between a flexible and creative child and one who, inspite of all learning, lacks the inner resources to apply his knowledge.

Lowenfeld, Viktor. *Creative and Mental Growth,* 3rd Edition. New York: MacMillan Co., 1957, p. 11.

For years, traditional school activities have centered around group learning. More progressive models of education are now encouraging the development of individualized activities. "Awareness of the Arts" presents a brief survey of useful art materials for a preschool program. Since these art materials are an integral part of the program, display them clearly, and once introduced into the program, make them easily accessible to children.

Art materials do not have to be used in any one way to be used "correctly." Children's art is more than painting and pasting. It is a means of individual expression and creativity. It is also a means of communicating ideas without words. Viewed in this way, any form of expression is acceptable. Young children learn skills through trial and error and positive reinforcement from peers and adults. The finished product often reveals only a portion of the variety of experiences the child has had along the way. With exploration comes confidence and freedom from pre-conceived standards.

Art Questionaire

Before continuing with this section, jot down some of your thoughts in response to the following questions. Share them with friends and colleagues.

1. Why do we include art in a curriculum for young children? What is the importance of including it at all?

2. How is working with art materials different from working with other things, for example: puzzles, games, or counting?

3. What aspect of a child's growth is most affected by work with art related activities? How can we, the adults who work with preschool children, make art experiences meaningful?

Brush Painting

Provide a large, comfortable, secluded area for painting. When possible, plan space so that the children are able to paint side by side instead of on opposite sides of the easel. Encourage communication while children are painting.

Purpose   To explore paint as an art media.

Procedure   Examine the brushes.
Experiment with the different ways brushes make strokes and the ways they can be used. Paint with the paper on the easel. Paint with the paper flat on the floor or on a table. Sit and stand while painting.

Which do you like and why?

Follow Up   Paint on:

Manilla paper	Cardboard
Construction paper	Corrugated paper
Easel paper	Old newspaper
Crepe paper	
Tissue paper	
Brown paper	

Use large sheets and give the children plenty of room so that they can expand the picture if they wish to do so.
Add some other papers to the list.

Procedure   Mixing paints:
Make orange from yellow and red.
Make purple from blue and red.
Make green from yellow and blue.
Experiment with pastels — name the colors that the children create and judge the qualities of the colors.

Write child's name, date, and anything he cares to tell you on his paper. Save pictures to put on display.

I love my grandmother and jaws.

Save paintings to make a scrapbook — one painting from each child per month. These paintings, correlated at the end of the school year, are a good measure of individual growth. They also give a pictorial history of the school year for the child and his family.

Other things to do with paint:
    Use as a coating for dried plants.
    Make potato and other vegetable paintings.
    Create wall hangings and materials.
    Fold into paper to make designs.

Finger Painting

Purpose

To develop a sense of touch and imaginative designs.

Finger paint gives children a direct tactile experience with paint. Final results are not important, but motor activity related to the experience is. Smearing is natural for children and should be provided for in children's activities. At first, children are cautious, using one finger and gingerly moving paint around. Be patient — it will not take long for them to be amply involved. Children enjoy this activity. It has its place in school art. Paint on the table tops, oil cloth, special finger painting paper and freezer paper.

Materials

Commercial Finger Paint:
    1. Finger paint paper
    2. Construction paper
    3. Shelf paper
Starch base finger paint sprinkled with powdered paint.
Starch base finger paint with food coloring.
Buttermilk finger paint.

Homemade Finger Paint:

Materials	1 cup water 1 T. boric acid
	½ cup sugar Liquid cloves
	1 cup flour

Procedure   Boil three cups of water in the top of a double boiler. Add mixture of sugar and flour and stir until hot. Remove from heat and add 1 T. boric acid powder and liquid cloves, as a preservative. Store in an airtight container.

Follow Up   Here are two additional types of finger paints. Each one is edible and delicious. Each expands the sensory awareness of finger painting from touch and sight to taste and smell.

Chocolate Pudding Finger Paint:

Materials   1 package instant chocolate pudding
water
egg beater
bowl
finger painting paper.

Procedure   Children prepare the chocolate pudding. Once prepared, use chocolate pudding just as you would any finger paint.

Karo Syrup Finger Painting:

Materials
    Corn Syrup
    Food Coloring
    Finger Painting Paper

Procedure
Place a tablespoon of corn syrup onto finger painting paper. Add a few drops of food coloring. Proceed as you would with regular finger painting. Paintings must be dried flat and left for several days — otherwise they will stick together.

RELATED COLOR ACTIVITIES

Color Dilution Trays
This activity is an inexpensive introduction to mixing and creating new colors from primary colors.

Materials
Color Dilution Trays — use 1" square plastic ice cube trays or plastic chemical trays available from chemical supply house.
    Food Coloring — All colors
    Plastic Eye Droppers
    Water
    Paper Towels

Procedure   Begin by filling each tray with water. Place a drop of one color of the food coloring in two of the diagonal corners of the tray. Give each child an eyedropper. By squeezing different amounts of color into each compartment of the tray, different shades of the same color are produced. Start with one color — increase to two or three. Dip paper towels into colored solutions and compare results.

Color Books

Materials   Lightweight oaktog (manilla folder weight)
One primary or secondary color of tempera paint
White tempera paint
Scissors
Paint brushes
Small containers
Paste

Procedure   Mix colored tempera paint with white paint adding different amounts of white as you go. When a variety of shades has been prepared, paint blobs of color onto oaktog. Cut out different shapes and paste them into a book. Name each shade: forest, mint, grass, candy cane, cotton candy, pink, sunshine, lemon yellow.

Modeling

CLAY
Purpose   To provide varied opportunity for small muscle development, imagination and dramatic play.

Clay has been used from early in recorded time to make works of art and useful objects. It is mainly used for sculpture. Children like to roll it, pound it and kneed it.

What can you and the children do with clay?

Procedure   Clay should be soft and malleable. If it is too hard, add water and let children wet their hands before using it.

Prepare the clay a few days before you use it by rolling fist fulls into balls, sticking your thumb into each ball and filling the space left by the thumb with water. Place all clayballs into an airtight covered plastic container or large plastic garbage bag which can be closed and sealed. Clay should be stored in this manner as well.

Follow Up   Without thinking of any special forms beforehand, what shapes can you make from the clay?

What can you do with a long coil of clay?

Does using utensils with clay help you? If so how?

PLAYDOUGH

Purpose To develop small muscle coordination through manmade modeling material.

Playdough is different than clay in texture. There are several kinds. Their uses are similar to those of natural clay. Playdough however is manmade, fun to prepare and decorate. Explore the differences between clay and playdough. Example: texture, color, smell. Record them.

Method A

Materials 1 cup water + 4 T. water
starch-used for heaviest solution as stated on package.

Procedure Prepare the starch and let stand for a few hours. Add food coloring.

Method B

Materials 1 cup salt
1 cup flour
½ cup water colored with food coloring

Procedure Add flour and salt to colored water stirring to avoid lumpiness. Add more flour if too sticky.

Follow Up Save playdough in covered plastic containers or jars with lids. Add decorations such as feathers, buttons, or pipe cleaners and let harden. Playdough can be baked in a moderate oven; 350°, and painted when cool.

SAWDUST MOLDING

Purpose To gain experience with another variety of modeling material.

Sawdust molding is a textured molding material. Exploration and initial preparation include:
Describing the texture of the sawdust and wallpaper paste, both dry and wet, mixing and molding, creating a puppet or prop for dramatic play areas.

Materials Wood shavings
Wall paper paste
Water
Plastic bucket

Procedure   Obtain sawdust from a lumber mill. It usually can be gotten free as shavings left over from cuttings of the day. Mix wallpaper paste following directions on the package, until it is a moderate consistency (about that of cookie dough). Slowly add sawdust and mix by hand until sawdust and paste form a ball.

Follow Up   Give each child a prepared sawdust ball. Add feathers, pipe cleaners and other collage material. Shape puppets, fruit and other dramatic play props. When the child has finished, place sawdust ball on paper towel and dry in a sunny place turning the product once a day to prevent sticking or mildew. Sawdust puppets will dry to a rocklike consistency. Material can be painted when dry. Think of other materials to add to the sawdust before it dries.

PAPER MACHE

Purpose   The purpose is the same as for other modeling material.

Materials   Newspaper
Flour
Water
Chicken wire for shaping if desired.

Preparation   **Method 1**

To make a mask or bird or animal:

1. Crumble large pieces of newspaper in the approximate shape of the desired mask or animal.
2. Tear newsprint into strips, about one inch wide. Tear along the grain of the paper to assure evenness. (If torn the "wrong" way" you will get jagged strips.) Help the children discover the "right" way to tear paper with the grain.
3. Mix paste with water.
4. Apply a layer of strips dipped in the paste to the form.
5. Add any protuberances (eye-brows, noses, or in the case of animals, legs and tails). Do this by crushing pieces of newspaper in the desired shape and attach them by putting paste strips over them.
6. Add five layers of pasted strips. It helps children to keep count of the layers if they put a layer of regular newspaper strips alternately with a layer of colored newspaper strips from comics.
7. Allow to dry.
8. Remove the paper core from a mask only.
9. Paint and decorate (decorations can be painted with poster paints. (Add collage materials.)

Method 2

1. Tear up newspaper into small pieces about 1" square.
2. Soak in water overnight.
3. Next day, mix flour and water and stir thoroughly. (This should be about the consistency of clay.)
4. Model animals, etc., as you would with clay. Only chunky animals are suitable to the material.
5. Paint and decorate with poster paint.

Follow Up   Paper maché is a good introduction to language arts experiences, story writing and puppet shows. What other experiences can you think of?

Collage

Purpose   To develop imaginative designs through use of varied materials.

Collage is the artful combination of natural and manmade materals on canvas, cardboard or other flat surface to form a unified design. Collage was first used in the early 1900's by famous artists like Picasso. Today it is one of the most popular art forms in the preschool classroom because if provides limitless, unstructured opportunities for collection and display of materials.

Materials

Cutting and Fastening:

Scissors	Elmer's Glue
Wire Cutters	Rubber Cement
Paper Punches	Flour and water paste
Paper clips	Wheat paper paste
Brads	Wire

Papers:

Corregated	Contact
Shiny	Tissue
Dull	Crepe
Newspaper	Cardboard
Wrapping	Wallpaper
Shelf	Cellophane
Sandpaper	

Fabric:

Smooth, scratchy, rough, bumpy

Fur	Corduroy	Nylon
Cotton	Velvet	Lace
Satin	Linen	Netting
Burlap	Sacking	Organdy

Transparent and semi-transparent chiffon

Natural Materials:

Bark	Seeds	Leaves
Dried Moss	Pods	Acorns

Sparkling and Shiny Materials:

Sequins (florists supply or 5 & 10 store)

Coinette ribbon (florists supply store)

Christmas tinsel

Aluminum foil (grocery store)

Metallic paper (art supply store or 5 & 10 store)

Shapes:

Buttons   Corks
Colored cellophane drinking straws
Bottle caps   Scrap sponge
Colored toothpicks
Tongue depressors and wooden applicators (druggist)
Colored cup cake cups
Fluted chocolate and cookie cups
Colored string and yarn
Gummed stickers, stars, arrows, etc.

Miscellaneous:

Egg cartons   Bottle caps
Cotton balls   Buttons
Pipe cleaners   Styrofoam
Wood scraps   Feathers
Netting or sacking

Construction and Mobiles

Materials Wire snips and pliers
Scissors
Staplers
Hammers
Many scrap materials can be used for construction and mobiles.
Wire coat hangers and many of the materials used for collage.
Dowels, 1/8" to 1/2".
Wire, various weights, from 16 to 24 gauge (in rolls at hardware store)
Wire, in cut lengths of 18" can be bought in boxes from florist supply house. (This is most economical and convenient. If three gauges are desired, get 16, 18 and 24)
Colored paper cut in long strips of various length.
Colored paper and metallic paper for children to cut into shapes.
Cardboard
String, colored
Metal foil
Items listed under "Collage."
For base:
> Clay, Cardboard, Composition board, Wood (attach wires with double tacks; staples from hardware store)

Tearing, Cutting and Pasting

Purpose   To develop small muscle dexterity.

Scissors are sometimes difficult for young children to manage —
especially if they are left handed. (Left-handed scissors never
seem to work.) Before cutting, plan tearing and pasting activities.
Next, paste precut paper. Finally, cut freehand designs and paste.

Materials   Scissors that work — both right and left handed.
Paper of all kinds
Soft material
Library paste
Elmer's Glue

Procedure   Simple:
Cut and paste torn free forms.
Cut and paste cut free forms.
Cut and paste pre-drawn forms.

These are more complicated free forms.
How do they work with preschoolers?
Can they fold and cut shadow images?

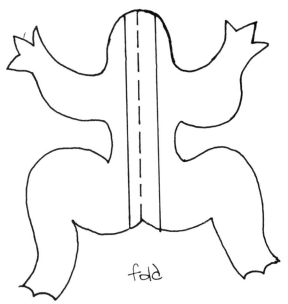

fold

Cut the paper in a design after folding it in half. Paste the design
on a thin sheet of paper (typing paper thickness). Move a light
up and down in back of paper. Figure shadows appear to dance.

Printing

Purpose   To explore a reproduceable art media.

Prints can be made with all types of natural as well as rubber material. As with the other art media, it is best to provide the necessary materials, letting children explore the variety of uses rather than structuring the experience rigidly. Linoleum and vegetable prints are two of the most popular printing activities for preschoolers.

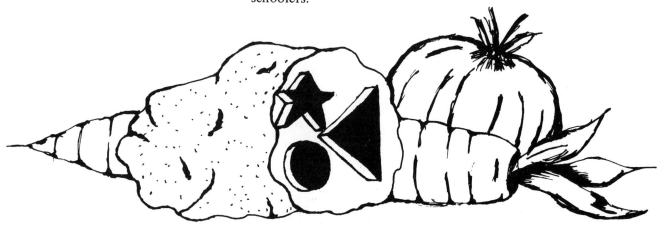

VEGETABLE PRINTING:

Materials
Vegetables	Baby food jar tops
Paring knife	Paper
Poster paint	Glass
Vaseline	Pencil
Paper - newsprint, construction, towel	

Procedure   Block printing can be done with cut out vegetables and fruits. This involves cutting a design in a carrot, onion, or potato. Mix poster paint and pour into the tops of baby food jars. Dip the vegetable into the paint and print on various papers.

GLASS PRINTING

Paint on glass or smooth surface by putting a layer of vaseline on the surface. Add powdered paint and roll with a brayer (a rubber roller on a handle) to mix. Put a piece of paper over this, and mark it with a moderately pointed pencil being careful not to pierce the paper. Pull paper off glass. Result will resemble a wood cut.

LINOLEUM BLOCK PRINTING

Materials

Gouges	To be bought in sets or individually.
Linoleum tiles	Check floor covering stores for reduced cost.
Water soluable inks	Art supply houses carry water soluable inks.
Papers	Try newsprint, paper towels, Japanese rice,
Brayers	or construction papers.
Glass — 6" x 6" or larger	Brayers — rolling pin, spoons also helpful.

Procedure

1. Children sketch a rough design on the linoleum tile.
2. They then gouge the areas of the tile where they do not want ink. They must learn correct technique of holding the gouge away from their hands and bodies.
3. When the tile has been thoroughly gouged leaving only the area which is to bear ink, children prepare the inks.
4. A small amount of ink (about a tablespoonful) is applied to a clean piece of glass (window panes are convenient). As the brayer is moved back and forth over the inked glass, the ink will be distributed evenly on the brayer.
5. When the tile has been dusted for any loose particles of linoleum, use the brayer to spread an even coating of ink on the tile. The ink should cover the raised areas thoroughly.
6. Place the linoleum tile upside down on the paper which the child has chosen and use a clean brayer to press the tile against the paper. A spoon or rolling pin is a good brayer which the child can bring from home. The child must be careful to hold the tile in place in order to prevent smudging of the ink.
7. The child then carefully lifts the tile from the paper which is then set away to dry.
8. All of the tools as well as the cut linoleum tiles can be washed with water and stored for future use.

NOTE: Blocks of wood can be glued to the backs of the linoleum tiles thus making the tile more permanent and easy to handle.

Color Media

COLORED CHALK

Lecturer's chalks (round or square) can be used wet or dry for drawing and interesting textured effects. Basic colors: black, white, red, yellow, blue, added: green (dark) purple, light orange pink, light blue and gray.

Alfa colored chalk is another type of chalk. It can be purchased in boxes of assorted colors.

CRAYPAS

Come in boxes of assorted colors, and are used on various textured papers.

CRAYONS

Special effects are created by melted crayons. Melt crayons in the top of a double boiler. Once in this fluid state, it has many uses such as decoration for paper mache or use to make features on puppets. Add melted crayon with either a drip technique or a brush.

Papers:
Same as for painting.

Puppets

Purpose To develop materials which can be used in dramatic and imaginative play.

Puppets are inanimate objects that are made to move by humans. They are and probably always will be a favorite of children. Dolls do not fall into this category but marionettes, puppets which look like dolls but move by the use of strings, do.

Procedure There are dozens of puppets to choose from.

Solid puppets. The head of this type is made from any solid object; apple, potato, carrot, or ball of tightly rolled newspaper. Any solid object will do as long as you can scoop it out. As a final step, drape a handkerchief over your hand and arm.

Sock puppets. Stuff the end of the sock with newspaper or cotton forming the head. Sew on the face and slip your hand into the open end of the sock. The puppet moves by bending your fingers.

Stick puppets. Draw a figure on a part of the stick or a thick piece of cardboard. Dress or cover both sides of the figure. Paste the puppet to the end of the slender stick so that the stick serves as a handle.

Paper Sack Puppets. Draw or paint a face on a bag. You can also paste pieces of paper on the bag. Cut a hole on either side of the bag for your fingers.

Carrot Puppets. Bore a hole in the widest part of the carrot so that the carrot will fit over your index finger. Paint or tack on features.

Eggshell Puppets. Carefully prick a hole in the end of an egg and make the hole bigger until your finger will fit inside.

Paper Maché and Sawdust puppets. The method of making these is the same as working and preparing the media that has already been described. See page 28.

PUPPET THEATRES

There are several kinds of puppet theatres.

Blanket Theatres. The theatre consists of a blanket or sheet which is stretched to any length desired. Fasten the ends to anything solid to hold it up. Puppeteers stand behind the blanket.

Table Theatre. The top of the table serves as the stage. Fasten a sheet to the top and let it hang to the floor.

Box Theatre. Find an oblong box and remove two of its sides. Stand on the other side and move puppets inside the box.

Selected References

Bland, Jane C. *Art of the Young Child.* New York: Museum of Modern Art, 1958.

Brommer, Gerald, F. *Wire Sculpture and Other Three Dimensional Construction.* Mass.: Davis, 1968.

Chernoff, Goldie T. *Clay, Dough, Play Dough.* Illustrated by Margaret A. Hartelius. School Book Service, 1974.

Cherry, Claire. *Creative Art for the Developing Child.* California: Fearon Publishers, 1972.

Cutler, Katherine, N. *From Petals to Pinecones.* Illustrated by Guilio Maestro. New York: Lothrop, 1969.

D'Amico, Victor. *Art for the Family.* New York: Museum of Modern Art, 1954.

Frankel, Lillian and Godfrey. *Creating from Scrap.* New York: Sterling, 1962.

Gilbert, Dorothy. *Can I Make One: A Craft Book for the Preschool Child.* New York: Transatlantic, 1970.

Johnson, Lillian. *Paper Maché.* New York: McKay, 1958.

Lewis, Shari. *The Tell It, Make It Book.* J. P. Tarcher, 1972.

Wiseman, Ann. *Making Things. The Handbook of Creative Discovery.* Boston: Little Brown & Co., 1973.

Lowenfeld, Viktor. *Creative and Mental Growth.* New York: Macmillan Co., 1957.

Marshall, Sybil. *An Experiment in Education.* Cambridge England: University Press, 1963.

Pile, Naomi. *Art Experiences for the Young Child.* Volume 5. Threshold Early Learning Library. New York: Macmillan Co., 1973.

Pluckrose, Henry. *Art: Informal Schools in Britain Today.* New York, Citation Press, 1972.

Razzi, James. *A Pop up Book of Fun and Easy Things to Make.* New York: Random House, 1975.

Read, Herbert. *Education Through Art.* New York: Pantheon Books, 1958.

part 3 / the song is love

Introduction
Experiences with Movement
Experiences with Chants, Finger Plays and Poems
Easily Constructed Musical Instruments
Selected References

Introduction

I've got a song, let me sing it with you
Let me say it now while the meaning is new
But wouldn't it be great if we could say it together
Don't be afraid to sing me your mind
Sing about the joys that I know we can find
Wind them around and see what they sound like together.
The song is love, the song is love, the song is love, the song is love.

> Dixon, Kniss, Stookey
> Yarrow, Travis

Music and movement are basic to all living things, becoming individual experiences for each person no matter what age. Children make contact with their world by exploration and use of their senses. Rhythmic expression is a part of dance as well as music. It includes stopping, starting, rest periods, activity, stress, softness and loudness. Rhythmic expression communicates inner feelings to others. The goals of the music and movement experiences presented in *Child's Play* are:

> To provide opportunities for children to explore their bodies in space;
> To develop a sense of body and coordination;
> To learn to move comfortably and confidently in the social world;
> And to channel the natural flow of emotional responses through movement.

Dixon, Kniss, Stookey, Yarrow, Travis. Peter Paul and Mary. *Album 1700*, Warner Brothers, S 39256. WS 1700.

Your role in providing expressive outlets for children's moods is to help them discover an inner self expression while learning to respect the expressive moods of others. Learning chants, finger plays and poems is part of the process as is learning to make instruments and move through space. Creative expression is at one of its highest peaks in the preschool years. Don't be afraid to sing your minds, hear and share the joys of children. "Wind them around and see what they sound like together. The song is love . . . ."

Experiences with Movement

Purpose   To familiarize children with basic rhythms:
4/4; 3/4; 2/4; 6/8.

Procedure   Children clap the rhythm or repeat what you do on a drum. Ask them to do the initial rhythm in double time. Ask them to do the initial rhythm in triple time.

Purpose   To familiarize children with patterns such as:
Long — Short Rhythms
Short — Long Rhythms

Follow Up   Move into other activities of locomotion. Walk in a group in time to the drum or the music — STOP! Run together — STOP!
Leap
Hop
Slide
Gallop, if possible
Skip, if possible

Procedure   Combine two rhythms and ask children to repeat the pattern, "long, long, long, short." This can be done by clapping or beating on a drum.

Purpose	To combine and compose small rhythmic sets.
Procedure	Adult gives directions such as, "walk, run, run, hop, hop, jump!" Children make up their own combinations and sets.
Purpose	To move in the following ways as the music quality suggests.
Procedure	Words are supplemented by patterns indicative of the movement:

swaying	vibrating	bending
swinging	exploding	stretching
rocking	striking	twisting
bouncing	relaxing	twirling
shaking	falling	turning

Follow Up	Add your own words to the list.
Purpose	To begin using different levels of space.
Procedure	Move up on tip-toes holding the body as high as possible. Move holding the body as low as possible. Move holding the body supported on one knee. Move holding the body supported on both knees.

EXERCISE WITH INSTRUMENTS

Purpose
To experiment with keeping steady rhythms repeating them over again using various instruments.

Procedure
Half of the group claps while the other half plays on instruments. The groups then switch.

Play patterns on drums which children repeat.

One child plays on instrument while group dances. Bells are good instruments for this activity.

Children select the instrument they wish to play.

Purpose
To express various moods through music.

Procedure
Select a piece of music which creates a certain mood. This can be classical or popular. Children describe the mood and then move in response to the music expressing whichever mood they have described. Here are some mood words to help get started.

gay	peaceful	angry
sad	noisy	fighting
sleepy	serious	comical
awake	lovingly	

Follow Up
Props provide a way of stimulating moods and facilitate acting out feelings to music. Here are some suggestions for props:

Display scarves, hats, and scrap material while telling the children to imagine they are in a fire and need to help each other escape. Help children identify each character. Act out the scene and then discuss feelings and emotions.

Display feathers on a table. Children select and blow the feathers into the air as they fall the children act out the movement of the feathers while you recite this poem.

I dearly love a floating feather,
A soft petal sailing by,
It weightlessly changes with the weather,
As the wind carries it to the sky.

Make up your own poems and incorporate the use of props.

Experiences with Chants, Finger Plays and Poems

RHYTHMIC CHANTS

Purpose   To introduce each child and adult to one another.

Procedure   While snapping fingers in 4/4 time, the leader and the group recite together:
>   Higglety pigglety, bumble bee,
>   Can you tell your name to me?

Child or adult responds in rhythm:
>   Cathy . . . . . Susan
Repeat around the group.

Follow Up   Chanting is a way to gather the group together. Add each child's name as he comes into the group.
>   Here we sit together, together, together,
>   Here we sit together on the floor.
>   Here's Susan and Jane and Billy and Tom . . .
>   Here we sit together on the floor.
Repeat until every one is present.

Purpose   To say goodbye to everyone in the group.

Procedure   Sing:
>   Goodbye everybody, yes indeed, yes indeed, yes indeed,
>   Goodbye everybody, yes indeed, yes indeed, my darling.

Sing:
>   So long it's been good to know you — Repeat three times.
>   I've got to be moving along.

I Dig Up the Dirt

I dig up the dirt, I dig up the sand
I am a steam shovel, that's what I am.

I carry away the dirt, I carry away the sand.
I am a dump truck, that's what I am.

I flatten down the dirt, I flatten down the sand.
I am a roller, that's what I am.

Purpose   To move the body in response to words in a rhythmic pattern.

Chug, Chug, Chug

Chug, chug, chug, chug tug boats work all day —
Repeat twice.
Push and pull the ocean liner, tug boats work all day —
Repeat twice.
Push and pull the other boats, tug boats work all day —
Repeat twice.

Procedure Children move like the boats in the song. Pair them and have
them move together.

Johnny Pounds with One Hammer

Johnny pounds with one hammer
One hammer, one hammer.
Johnny pounds with one hammer all day long.

Procedure Begin song by moving one fist.
Move two fists and say, "Johnny works with 2 hammers, etc. . . .
Move two fists and one foot and say, "Johnny works with three
hammers, etc. . . .
Move two fists and two feet and say, "Johnny works with four
hammers, etc. . . .
Move two fists, two feet and head and say, "Johnny works with
five hammers, etc. . . .

Now Let's Get the Rhythm

Now let's get the rhythm with the head	Ding Dong	(Shake head)
Now let's get the rhythm with the hands	Clap Clap	(Clap hands)
Now let's get the rhythm with the feet	Stamp Stamp	(Stamp feet)
Now let's get the rhythm with the hips	Hot Dog	(Swing hips)
Now let's get the rhythm again.	Repeat	(Ding Dong)
		(Clap Clap)

Procedure   Start chant slowly and pick up speed as you go.

(Stamp Stamp)

(Hot Dog)

Speak softly

Keep calm, keep calm
Watch your step
Look before you   LEAP!

Procedure   Start in a crouched position. Look around slowly and then LEAP up.

FINGER PLAYS

Here's a Ball

Here's a ball
And here's a ball
And a great big ball I see
Shall we count them all again — 1, 2, 3.

Procedure   Make three imaginary balls. Start with a small ball by using hands and then move a large one by stretching arms in a rounded position above the head.

Flickety, Flickety, Flack

Flickety, flickety flack — Repeat twice.
The wipers on the car go flickety, flickety, flack
The wipers go flick and the wipers go flack,
Flickety, flickety flack. — Repeat twice.

Procedure   Move hands back and forth together as the windshield wipers on the car. Keep in rhythm with the words.

Swimming, Swimming, Swimming

Swimming, swimming in the swimming pool,
When days are hot, when days are cold,
In the swimming pool,
Breast stroke, side stroke, fancy diving too,
Oh, don't you wish you had nothing else to do
BUT!

Procedure Repeat the chant three times.
First time put motions and words together.
Second time Hum and do motions.
Third time only do motions.
At the end of each chant, yell! — "But" as a group.

Apple Tree Song

Way up high in the apple tree,
Two little apples sat smiling at me,
I shook the tree as hard as I could,
Down came the apples — mmmm they were good!

Procedure Point up in the tree. Hold up two fingers for the two apples.
Shake the imaginary tree. Move hands in a wavy motion to
indicate falling apples.

FAMILIAR CHILDREN'S POEMS

Pat-a-cake, pat-a-cake bakers man
Bake me a cake as fast as you can.

Wina dena dina dum,
Cattana wina wina wum
Spit spot must be done
Twiddle and twoddle and twenty one.

Little Tommy Tucker
Sings for his supper.
What shall we give him
Brown bread and butter?
How shall he cut it without a knife?
How shall he marry without ere a wife?

Wee Willie Winkle runs through the town
Upstairs and downstairs in his nightgown.
Rapping at the window,
Crying through the lock.
Are the children in their beds?
It's past eight o'clock.

Cry baby bunting
Daddy's gone a hunting
To catch a little rabbit skin
To wrap our baby bunting in.

Ring a round of rosie
Pocket full of posies
Ashes, ashes, we all fall down.

Tom Tom the pipers son
Stole a pig and away did run
Pig was eat, eat, eat
Tom Tom Tom was beat, beat, beat
And Tom went roaring, roaring, roaring
Down the street, street, street.

My little pony needs some shoes
How many nails must I use?
1, 2, 3 tie him to a tree
Let him have a bag of hay
Then he will not run away.

I hear thunder — Repeat twice.
So do you — Repeat twice.
Pitter Patter rain drops — Repeat twice.
I'm wet through, so are you.

My little sports car needs some gas
How many dollars shall I ask
Raise the hood, check the oil
I'll be back in a very short while.

Little Boy Blue, Come Blow Your Horn.

It's raining, it's pouring,
The old man is snoring.
Bumped his head and
Went to bed and
Couldn't get up in the morning.
Rain, rain go away,
Come again some other day.
Little . . . . wants to play.

I'm waitin' for you train
I'm waitin' for you now
I'm waitin' for you train
I'm waitin' for you now.

Come on you silly train
Why do you go so slow?
I know you're in there you train
I know you're there, I know.

Repeat this twice, getting louder and louder. Then
slow down to a whisper.

The baker is baking sweet bisquits so small
His oven will hold 700 in all.
Buy some for tea.
Buy some for tea.
The biggest for me.
The biggest for me.

The ducks in the pond go quack, quack, quack;
Naughty little ducklings, smack, smack, smack.
The big brown cow goes moo, moo, moo;
Milk for me and you, you, you.
The noisy little dogs go bark, bark, bark;
In the street and park, park, park.
Oink oink, oink goes the pig, pig, pig;
Looking for his food, dig, dig, dig.
Horse in the field goes nay, nay, nay;
Eats grass and hay, hay, hay.
Donkeys go he haw, he haw;
Likes to lie on straw, straw, straw.

Duck, duck, duck — quack, quack, quack.
Big blocks, small blocks — stack, stack, stack.
Cow cow cow — moo, moo, moo,
Sticky sticky fingers — glue, glue, glue.
Dog, dog, dog — bark, bark, bark.
Off go the lights — dark, dark, dark.

Dance to your daddy my little laddie.
Dance to your daddy my little man.
You shall have a fishy on a little dishy.
Dance to your daddy my little bonnie man.

Easily Constructed Musical Instruments

Drum

Materials Tin cans (with and without lids), cardboard containers and boxes, bits of inner tubing, small tacks or nails, colored paper, glue, scissors (for decorating)

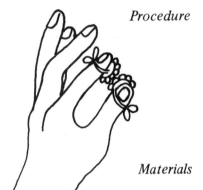

Procedure Decorate the various-sized tubes and cans. Stretch pieces of tubing across tops of lid-less containers — secure the tubing with small tacks.

For drumsticks; use clothespins, pencils, (eraser end) and sticks — hands work fine too!

Rattles

Materials Small jars and lidded containers, paper bags; dried peas, beans, macaroni — anything that rattles.

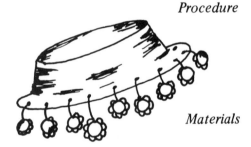

Procedure Fill containers with various materials. Secure lids on jars and boxes. Blow up bags and drop in beans or seeds. Twist top and tie tightly. Decorate the bag and shake.

Tambourines

Materials Pie tins or similiar aluminum containers, wire or string, small bells or bottle caps, paper punch or hammer and nail.

Procedure Flatten bottle caps, punch holes in center with nail. Make loops with thread, fasten to fingers and clack together.

Wood Blocks

Materials Two small blocks of wood, small pieces of sandpaper, tacks or staples, empty thread spools.

Procedure Stretch sandpaper across one side of wood block; secure with tacks. Glue or nail spool on the opposite side of block for a handle. Rub blocks together, experimenting with different rhythms.

String Instruments

Materials   Lidded boxes and cylindrical containers, thread (of varying materials and weights), corks (or similar objects). Rubber bands (all sizes) bits of wood or cardboard, glue, scissors or matte knife, long strips of wood, plastic or similar sturdy materials.

Procedure   For a very simple "strummer" cut small slits on opposite sides of a fairly shallow cardboard box, at regular intervals from each other. Stretch different sized rubber bands. Secure them in the slits. Then strum, or pluck the "strings" individually. Each one makes a different tone!

More String Instruments –

Materials   The same basic materials as for other string instruments.

Procedure   For a simple "banjo," take a lidded box and cut a round hole in the center of the lid. Glue two or more corks on the lid, just below the hole. Make a slit in the box at the top, just big enough to insert a metal or wooden "neck." Glue corks to the top, and, when dry, stretch thread or rubber bands between the corks (for strings). To increase tension, slip a "bridge," made of cardboard or wood, underneath the strings just above the center hole. Strum or pluck the strings to give varied tones.

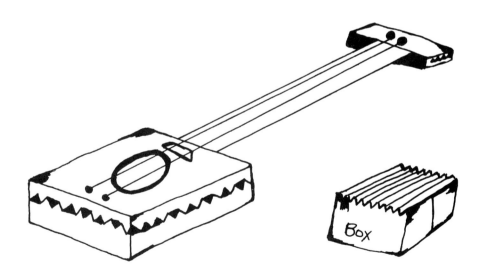

Bells and Chimes

Materials 8 glasses or bottles of a uniform size, several different "mallets," such as wooden or metal spoons.

Procedure Fill the glasses with varying amounts of water. Each one produces a different tone when struck with a mallet. You can even play a melody!

If you can suspend the glasses or bottles from some sort of frame, the tones will be completely different.

Simple Wind Chime

Materials Popsicle stick, tongue depressor, or similar flat piece, various sizes of nails, nylon string or thread, hammer and small nail.

Procedure Make holes across the stick and suspend nails. The tones will amaze you!

Kazoos

Materials Cardboard tubes, (toilet paper tubes, toweling tubes, tin foil tubes) Small pieces of wax paper, rubber bands or tape; colored paper or felt pens for decorating.

Procedure Cover both ends of the tube with wax paper and secure with rubber bands. Punch holes down the side of the tube. Hum or "toot" into one end of the tube. (It takes practice.)

Comb Kazoos

Materials Combs, wax paper, rubber bands or tape.

Procedure Cover comb on both sides with wax paper, fasten with rubber bands or tape. Hold comb to your mouth and hum a tune.

Selected References

Andrews, Frances M. *Sing Together Children*. Ohio: Cooperative Recreation Service Inc., 1960.

Aronoff, F. W. *Music and Young Children*. New York: Holt, Reinhart & Winston, 1969.

Flores, J. A. (ed.) *Songs and Dreams*. Connecticut: Pendulum Press, 1972.

Hawkinson, John & Faulhaber, Martha. *Music and Instruments for Children to Make*. New York: Scholastic Book Service, 1969.

Horton, John. *Music: Informal Schools in Britain Today*. New York: Citation Press, 1972.

Landeck, Beatrice. *Songs to Grow on*. New York: Edward B. Marks Music Corporation, 1950.

—————, *More Songs to Grow on*. New York: Edward B. Marks Music Corporation, 1954.

Landeck, Beatrice, Crook, Elizabeth. *Wake Up and Sing*. New York: Edward B. Marks Music Corporation, 1969.

Lomax, Alan. *The Folksongs of North America*. Carden City, N.Y.: Doubleday, 1960.

Milne, A.A., Simson, H. Fraser. *The Pooh Song Book*. New York: E. P. Dutton and Co., 1961.

Thomas, Marlo, et. al. *Free to Be You and Me*. New York: McGraw Hill, 1974.

Sexton, Jeanette, Clark, Steven. *Fun, Frolic and Frolic Songs*. Ohio: Willis Music Co.

—————, *Songs Children Like*. Washington D.C.: Association for Childhood Education International.

Seeger, Ruth C. *American Folk Songs for Children*. Illustrated by Barbara Cooney. New York: Doubleday, 1953.

part 4 / one two buckle my shoe

Introduction
One to One Correspondence
Numerals
Sets and Classification
Geometric Shapes and their Relationship
Ordering
Measuring
Selected References

Introduction

One Two, buckle my shoe, three four,
Close the door, five six, pick up sticks,
Seven eight, close the gate, nine ten,
Do it again.

Children actively manipulate materials to see how they work. They explore relationships between objects by touching, feeling, turning, pushing, pulling and sliding them. In doing so, they gain an understanding of mathematical concepts; internally consistent systems of organization and relationships.

Mathematical concepts are found in every part of preschoolers experiences. They include quantity, size, numbers, space and time. Consider block building. Blocks teach the concepts of bigger than, smaller than, more than, less than, longer than, and higher than. When used in the context of building structures, these terms have vivid and concrete meaning for children. Unit blocks promote these concepts. They are designed in multiples of half units, units, double units, circles, half circles and cylindars.

Number is another mathematical concept for preschool children. It too is a part of the everyday preschool experience. Every member of the group has one chair, every person gets one napkin and one cup at lunch. This number concept is referred to as one-to-one correspondence.

Another mathematical concept for preschool children is measurement. Measurement offers the opportunity to compare height, weight, volume and time.

This chapter of *Child's Play* presents the following mathematical concepts:

One-to-one correspondence
Numerals
Sets and classification
Geometric shapes and their relationships
Ordering
Measuring

A mathematical vocabulary including words such as few, many, high, low, least, narrow, half, wide, shallow, deep, belonging to, different than and the same as, develops hand in hand with the practical experiences. Therefore, allow children to verbalize their discoveries. Focus on understanding the implications of each new learning experience and present unique opportunities for manipulation and exploration.

One to One Correspondence

Purpose   To understand that numerals stand for a class of things.

PUZZLE CARDS

Materials   Cardboard
Buttons, bottle caps, peas, beans
Scissors
Glue
Felt pens
Felt

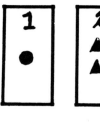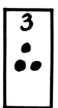

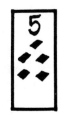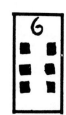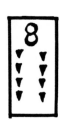

Procedure	To design a simple set of number cards, cut cardboard into 10 uniform pieces and place the numbers 1-10 consecutively on each piece. Mount the corresponding number of objects on each card. Match the right number of objects to the correct numeral.
Follow Up	Additional perception skills are provided by cutting the area around the number.

Follow Up	Cut a sliding piece out of the top of each card. Mount the cards on a sheet of sturdy cardboard and write the numeral underneath the sliding piece.

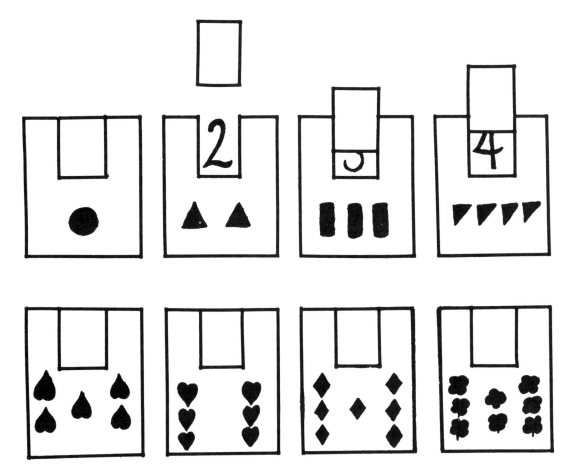

DOMINOES

Materials   Sturdy cardboard
Felt pens
Ruler
Scrap wood pieces cut into
uniform rectangles
Glue

Procedure   Create giant dominoes by placing symetrical designs on one or both sides of rectangular pieces of cardboard which have been divided in half by a felt pen. Draw numerals on some on the halves. The numeral that you draw and the number of objects that appear on each card do not have to match. Glue the cardboard designs to the individual blocks of wood. Play the domino game by having each child select a number of wood blocks and stand them up in front of him. Taking turns, each child matches the appropriate number of objects on his domino to a numeral he sees on the table. The game is completed when all the blocks are matched.

STRING BOARD

Materials   Heavy cardboard, matboard or a piece of plywood.
Various colors of yarn
Cup hooks, screw eyes, washers.
Wood is glued onto heavy cardboard to form a U.
Matboard is cut to fit between the slots in the wood.

Procedure   Matching pairs of pictures and numerals are written on two sets of cards. Screw eyes are attached to one side of the wood adjacent to the numbers on the cards. Cup hooks are attached in the

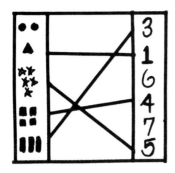

same manner on the other side. Yarn with washers on the ends are attached to the screw eyes when making a match. Child places the washer on the cuphook that is next to the numeral that matches the one the yarn is attached to. Pictures connect to corresponding numbers. Cards are interchangeable and can be made applicable for science, language arts, and other math activities as well.

PICK UP STICKS

Materials   Popsicle sticks numbered from one to ten.
Cut out felt shapes.
Juice can
Contact paper

Procedure   The numbered popsicle sticks are placed in a juice can with the numbers upward. The child selects a popsicle stick and picks the appropriate number of felt pieces to correspond to the number on the stick.

Numerals

Children learn number and size in relation to things they already know. Two objects are more than one. Two objects are less than three. Numerals are the written symbol for numbers. The symbol 4 is shorthand for 4 objects. Numerals become meaningful after children have had experience related to counting and matching. This has been referred to as one-to-one correspondence. Once one-to-one correspondence has been introduced, concentrate on recognition of the numeral on its own.

Materials   Peas
Beans
Buttons

Procedure   Put several groups of a number of small objects on the table. Ask children to arrange them in as many different patterns as they can. Conclude by asking them to shape the numeral itself.

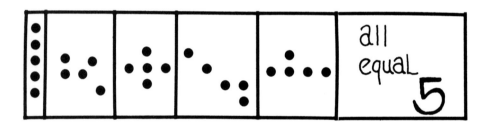

Materials   Sand paper
Wood blocks
Scissors
Glue

Procedure   Cut numerals out of sand paper and glue them onto wooden blocks. Children trace the numerals with their fingers repeating the name of the numeral.

Variation:

Materials   Sand
Coffee grounds
Baking tins

Procedure   Place grainy material in a shallow baking tin. Children trace numerals with their fingers.

NUMBER SONGS AND FINGER PLAYS

Materials Large cut numerals

Procedure Point to displayed numerals as they are referred to in individual songs and fingerplays. The following are well known number songs.

5 big cows standing in the barn
Standing in the barn — Repeat Twice.
5 big cows standing in the barn
Moo, moo, moo.

4 little ducks swimming in the pond — etc.
3 fat pigs walking in the mud
2 noisy dogs barking in the park
1 slippery snake sliding in the grass

1 man went to mow, went to mow a meadow
1 man and his dog went to mow a meadow
2 men went to mow, went to mow a meadow
2 men, 1 man and his dog went to mow a meadow
3 men went to mow, etc.

10 green bottles hanging on the wall — Repeat Twice
And if one of the bottles should happen to fall
There'll be nine green bottles hanging on the wall, etc.

Said like a poem, children show you with their hands:
Small ball, medium ball, big ball I see
I can count them, one, two, three
Repeat two or three times.

This Old Man, he played one
He played nick nack on my thumb.

With a nick nack, patty wack
Give your dog a bone.
This Old Man came rolling home.   [Chorus]

This Old Man he played two
He played nick nack on my shoe.

Three — on my knee
Four — at the door
Five — on my hide
Six — on my sticks
Seven — up in heaven
Eight — at the gate
Nine — on my spine
Ten — once again.

One, two, buckle my shoe
Three, four, close the door
Five, six, pick up sticks
Seven, eight, close the gate
Nine, ten, once again.

One little, two little, three little Indians
Four little, five little, six little Indians
Seven little, eight little, nine little Indians
Ten little Indian boys.

I see one, two, three
Three little bunnies reading the funnies
I see four, five, six
Six little men picking up bricks.

Five little chickadees sitting on a door
(hold up five fingers)
One flew away and then there were four
(put one finger down)
Chickadee, Chickadee, happy and gay
Chickadee, chickadee fly away
Four little chickadees on a tree
One flew away and then there were three.

Sets and Classification

Purpose   To understand a set is a collection of matchable things and ideas that share one or more of the same attributes.

ATTRIBUTE CARDS

Materials   Heavy cardboard
Scissors
Colored magic markers
String

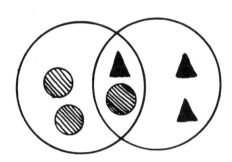

Procedure   Cut cardboard into various shapes sizes and color them with various colors. Make 40-50 cards. Place them on the table in a random manner. Arrange string to form three circles on the table. Beginning with one child, select a card and place it on the table within one of the string circles.
A second child is asked to select a card and place it on the table. If he sees an attribute that matches the first card he can place the card within the same circle as the first one. If nothing matches he places the card in the second string. Sometimes a card will share two attributes. In that case, overlap the strings and place the card in the space where the string overlaps. Continue this process until all the cards are used up. Discuss characteristics of the sets formed.

SET LOTTO

Materials   Any matchable items (for example):
        Comb, brush, toothpaste
        Macaroni, peas, beans
        Buttons, zipper, snaps
        Spools of thread, pins, yarn
    Cardboard
    Glue
    Magazine pictures

Procedure   Design a set of cards each one having its own theme. Possible themes include, grooming, sewing, fastening, things to eat.

To play the game, one person acts as caller and distributes cards to all the players. Three other players select items individually from a box into which they cannot see. They attempt to match objects they select from the box to the ones on their card. The first person to match all the items on his card with the ones selected from the box wins.

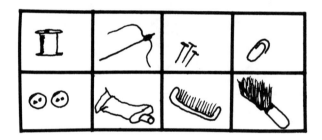

CLASSIFICATION

Materials   Articles of clothing such as:

sleeves	pants	Clothes pins
buttons	hats	Cardboard
zippers		Boxes
mittens		Brads
socks		

Procedure   Draw large cardboard figures that are actual life size. Make arms, legs, head, moveable by using brads to connect the body parts. Pin the bodies onto a large bulletin board. Have the children sort clothing into the appropriate boxes by occasion for each item of clothing. For example, articles of clothing appropriate for outdoors, indoors, sleeping, dress up, winter, summer.

Follow Up	This exercise can be adapted to clothing which a mother, a father, a brother, a sister, an infant could wear. Modify this activity further in classifying things that are found in different parts of the house: kitchen, bedroom, living room and playroom.

SORTING, GROUPING AND CLASSIFYING

Materials	Buttons, shells, matchboxes, pebbles, nuts, corks, marbles, bottle caps, stones, straws, beads, beans, laces, spools, colored sticks, playing cards, dice, egg cartons, variously sized containers, partitioned boxes.
Procedure	Sort, group and classify the above objects by size, color, shape, amount, thickness, thinness or any other means which you and the children devise.
Follow Up	Write numerals 1-12 on the bottom of egg cartons. Give a supply of objects to be counted to each child. As the child sorts the objects in front of him, have him place the proper amount of items in each of the numbered sections of the carton.

Things are called sets if they belong to a collection. Can these collections be sorted in any other way? |
| *Materials* | Large lined paper
Magic markers
Empty boxes
Items in the classroom |
| *Procedure* | Sort things according to the following criteria: |

Things that I like	Things that I don't like.
Things that are soft	Things that are hard.
Things that are large	Things that are small.
Things that are bright	Things that are dull.
Things that are long	Things that are short.
Things that float	Things that sink.

Geometric Shapes and Their Relationships

Purpose   To recognize basic geometric shapes and to perceive two or
more objects which have some relationship to one another.

CARDBOARD SQUARES

Materials   Cardboard
Ruler
Magic Marker

Procedure   Design a set of various sized squares cut out of cardboard. Make
them different colors. Draw a large square on a sheet of cardboard. The object of the activity is to see how many of the small
squares can be fitted into the larger one.

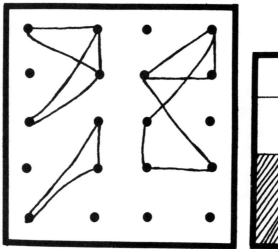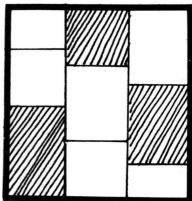

GEOBOARDS

Materials   Large square of ¼" plywood
Ruler
Small nails with heads
Rubber bands
5 x 8 cards with geometric shapes and the names of the shapes

Procedure   Mark a square plywood board into ½" squares. Nail small nails
into the intersection of the lines. Place a pile of rubber bands
on the table in front of the geoboards. Ask the child to see how
many different geometric shapes he can make by stretching the
rubber bands over the nails.

How many shapes can be placed on this board at the same time? How many things can you find in the classroom that are similar in shape to the shapes that are on the geoboard?

TANGRAM

A tangram is an ancient chinese puzzle cut from a square into five small triangles, a small square and a parallelogram. The object of the tangram is to remake the square using all the smaller pieces of the puzzle. Adults might have to draw puzzles for children to cut out. It is a challenge to give older children directions for drawing the puzzle as well.

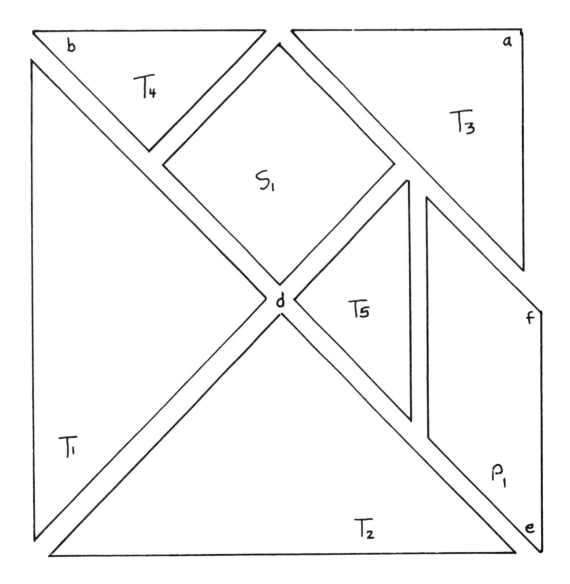

Materials	Ruler
	Tagboard
	Pencil
	Scissor

| Procedure | Follow procedure using Illustration No. 1 as a guide. |

Cut a six inch square from a piece of tagboard.

Fold the square on the diagonal.

Cut along the folded line producing two triangles.

Working with one of the large triangles, cut it in half and label the pieces T-1 and T-2. Lay those pieces aside.

Label points a, b, c, d, e and f as indicated on the illustration.

Take second large triangle and fold point a to point d (midpoint of the base of the triangle). Cut along the folded line and label triangle T-3.

Take remaining trapezoid. Fold point b to point d. Cut. Fold point e to point f. Cut along folded line to form T-4 and S-1.

Fold point d to point f and cut along the folded line forming T-5 and P-1.

Try putting the puzzle together again.

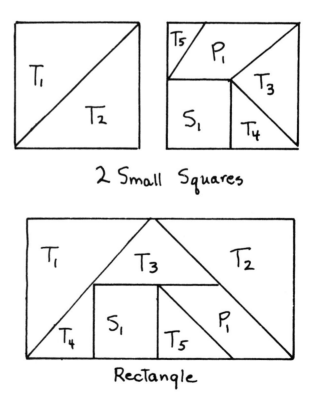

2 Small Squares

Rectangle

Follow Up   Make rectangle and two small squares out of the 7 tangram pieces. Make a rectangle by moving the fewest amount of pieces. How many moves did it take? See how many designs you can make with the tangrams using the illustrations as a guide.

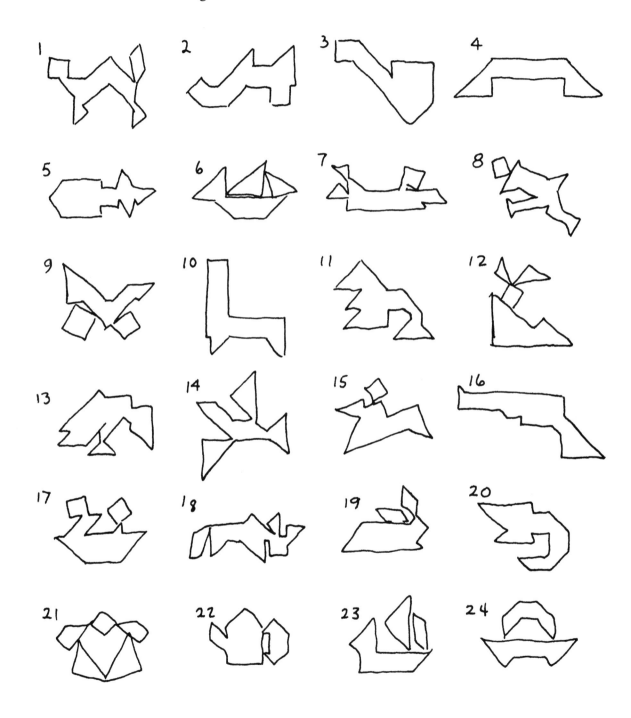

BLOCK BUILDING

Materials Unit Blocks: Properly labeled storage areas with pictures representing the size block to be stored.

Procedure Following are mathematical experiences related to block building.
Find the shortest block, the largest block, the tallest block, the curviest block.

Pile 1, 2, 3, 4, 5 blocks of the same shape on top of one another.

How many ways can you make piles of 2, 3, 4 and 5?

How many blocks can you pile before they fall?

How many short blocks does it take to make a long block, a medium sized block?

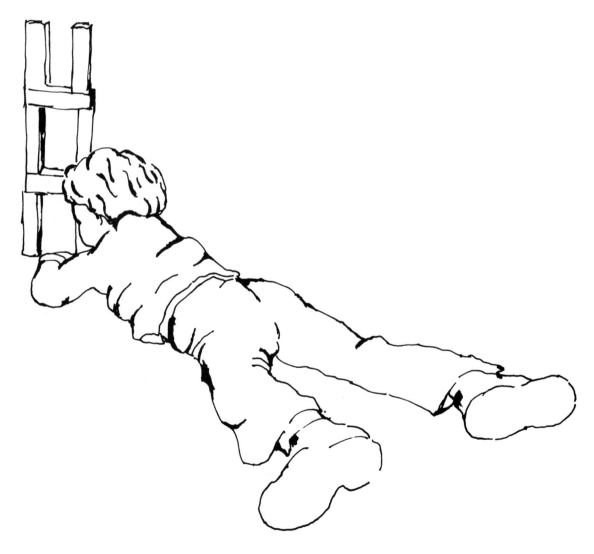

Ordering

Purpose   To perceive differences in size, and shape of objects for the purpose of placing them in ascending and descending order.

Materials   Cardboard rolls of different sizes
Can, boxes, blocks, rings

Procedure   Place an assortment of materials on the table in front of the child. Ask him to arrange them in any pattern he wishes and then from largest to smallest and smallest to largest.

Follow Up   Using the same materials, order them by height, length, and width. Begin with two or three objects at a time and work up to more.

COPYING PATTERNS

Materials   3 x 5 cards
Colored magic markers

Procedure   Draw patterns of geometric shapes on unlined three by five cards. Give children blank 3 x 5 cards and ask them to repeat the patterns found on the cards.

Follow Up   An extention of copying patterns is copying incomplete patterns and adding the missing similar shape needed to complete the pattern design.

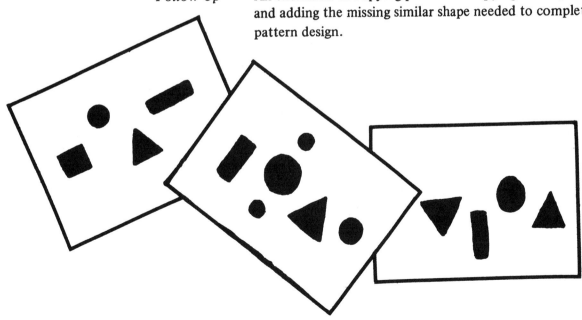

Hands and Feet

Materials

Materials Brown wrapping paper
Felt pieces
Wooden board
Scissors
Glue

Procedure Trace each child's hands and feet on sheets of brown paper. Trace the hands and feet of adults in the room as well. Arrange them in order from smallest to largest. Using brown paper as a pattern, cut the hands and feet out of felt and arrange them in the same ascending or descending order of size on the wooden board. Place felt board in the room so children can compare the relative size of their hands and feet. Record their observations.

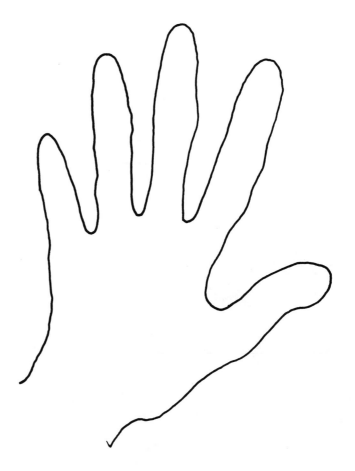

Measuring

Purpose To understand measurement in quantifiable terms.

GRAPHING

Materials Colored construction paper
Yard stick
Pencils

Procedure Children in the room measure each other. Heights are recorded by the adults or children if they are able to do so. Heights are tallied and similar ones are recorded on a bar graph to represent the relative heights of all the children in the room.

Follow Up Many things in your room can be counted and graphed. Here are a few examples:
Number of boys
Number of girls
Number of blocks
Number of red items
Number of blue items

How Long is It?

Materials   3 x 5 cards
Pencils
Blocks
Yarn
Straight edge measuring devices

Procedure   Distribute various measuring devices among the children. There should be a variety of materials for measuring. Try not to duplicate the measuring instruments. Send the children to measure various things in the room for example a table top, the floor, parts of walls, a block shelf. Record the various measurements and compare the results of the different measuring devices used. Example: a table top equals two lengths of yarn and 3 file cards. A table top also equals five unit blocks.

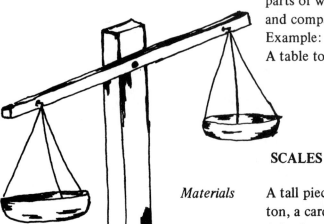

SCALES

Materials   A tall piece of wood or any other vertical piece, i.e., a milk carton, a cardboard tube.
A horizontal strip of wood
String
A thumb tack or nail
Two pie plates

Procedure   Punch holes in each end of the horizontal wooden strip. Attach it to the vertical beam with the nail. Punch holes in three sides of each pie plate. Attach the pie plates to the vertical bar with string. Weigh beans, beads, rice and any other small object.

Follow Up
Materials   Baby scale
Supermarket scale
Vegetable scale
Bathroom scale
Various items to weigh

Procedure   Provide a variety of materials to be weighed by a variety of scales. Record observations. Keep a chart of the items that have been weighed.

WATER PLAY

Materials   Containers of various sizes
A water table, sink or basin
Rubber tubing

Procedure   Using small containers, estimate the number of containers required to fill larger ones. Then test by actually filling containers with water. How close were your estimates?

Follow Up   Arrange the containers in order of size. Describe how they were arranged. (Smallest to largest, thinnest to fattest)

Some containers hold more water than others. How do children compare the differences? Are they able to tell that it takes two small ones to fill one large one? Can they tell that a short wide container might hold more water than a tall narrow one?

Some Water Play Materials
Containers: Any large containers that hold water.

Equipment:
Empty tins and bottles varying in size from soda to medicine.

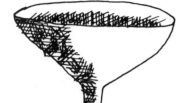

Funnels; bought or made from cardboard.

Tins with one large hole punched through the end.

Tins with very small holes punched in the middle of the closed end.

Tins with large holes punched in the end to act as a spray.

Tins with holes of two different sizes punched into closed end.

Tins with holes punched in the side.

A box of objects for sinking and floating: twigs, odd pieces of wood, nails, various odd pieces of sticks, stones, pods, corks, spools.

Plastic hosing of different lengths and widths. Hospitals are a good source for this.

Sponges of assorted sizes.

Plastic ice cube trays molded out of one piece of plastic.

Selected References

Adler, David. *3D, 2D, 1D.* Illustrated by the Author. New York: T.Y. Crowell, 1975.

Asimov, Isaac. *Numbers: A clear, imaginative approach to mathematics.* Boston: Houghton Mifflin Co., 1959.

Carini, Edward. *Take Another Look.* Englewood Cliffs, N.J.: Prentice Hall, Inc., 1971.

Dennis, J. Richard. Illustrated by Donald Crews. *Fractions are a Part of Things.* New York: Thomas Y. Crowell Co., 1971.

Eby, Carol; Kaup, Rachel; Lader, Estelle. *Fostering Growth in Mathematical Skills and Scientific Inquiry.* Darien, Conn.: Teachers Publishing Corporation, The Threshold Program for Early Learning, 1970.

Freeman, Mae. *Finding Out About Shapes.* Illustrated by Bill Morrison. New York: McGraw Hill, 1969.

Froman, Robert. *A Game of Functions.* Illustrated by Enrico Arno. New York: Thomas Y. Crowell, 1974.

Hirsch, Elizabeth S. ed. *The Block Book.* Washington, D.C.: National Association for the Education of Young Children, 1974.

Kahn, Selma. *Math Magic.* Atlanta, Ga.: Humanics Press, 1976.

Kline, Morris. *Mathematics, A Cultural Approach.* Reading, Mass.: Addison Wesley Publishing Co., 1962.

Lavatelli, Celia Standler. *Piaget's Theory Applied to Early Childhood Curriculum.* Boston: American Science and Engineering, 1970.

Meserve & Sobel. *Introduction to Mathematics.* Englewood Cliffs, N.J.: Prentice Hall, 1964.

Nuffield Foundation. *Mathematics Begins.* London: Newgate Press Ltd., 1967.

——————, *Pictorial Representation.* London: Newgate Press Ltd., 1967.

——————, *Computation and Structure 2.* London: Newgate Press Ltd., 1967.

——————, Nuffield Mathematics Project, *Environmental Geometry.* New York: John Wiley and Sons Inc., 1969.

——————, Nuffield Mathematics Project, *Shape and Size 2.* New York: John Wiley and Sons, Inc., 1969.

O'Brien, Thomas. Illustrated by Allan Eitzen. *Odds and Evens.* New York: Thomas Y. Crowell, Co., 1971.

Piaget, Jean. *The Child's Conception of Number.* New York: The Humanities Press, 1952.

Razzell, Arthur G., Watts, K. G. O. *This is 4: The Idea of Number.* Garden City, N.Y.: Doubleday & Co., 1964.

Russell, Solveig Paulson. Illustrated by Arnold Spilka. *Lines and Shapes: A First Look at Geometry.* New York: Henry Z. Walck Inc., 1965.

Schatz, Esther E., Wilsberg, Mary E. *Freeing the Learner in Primary Arithmetic.* Columbus, Ohio: College of Education, Ohio State University, 1964.

Spencer, Peter Lincoln, Brydegaard, Marguerite. *Building Mathematical Concepts in the Elementary School.* New York: Henry Holt & Co., 1952.

Trivett, Daphne Harwood. *Shadow Geometry.* Illustrated by Henry Roth. New York: Thomas Y. Crowell, 1974.

part 5 / a time for words

Introduction
Speaking
Listening
Reading
Writing
Discrimination and Recognition
Selected References

Introduction

Eyes are for seeing . . . . Ears are for hearing . . . . The mouth is for talking . . . . and the navel? . . . . is for what? Must be for beauty . . . ."

Preschooler
From Two to Five

Language is any means of communication that expresses feeling and thought. It is a main index of culture and an educational concern at all levels. Children communicate in a number of different ways, only one of which is verbal. Even the shyest child says something with an anxious look, nod or smile.

It is rare that children come to school without some form of verbal communication. Each child brings a set of highly personalized experiences with him which eventually contribute to his reading and writing skills. At the same time, however, he is developing speaking and listening skills. It is these four elements: speaking, listening, prereading and writing that are addressed in this chapter of *Child's Play*.

Why is language essential? First, language aids in the development of a positive self image. Part of experiencing success in any phase of life is understanding "Who I am." Communication solidifies these feelings. Second, language provides a way to make feelings and thoughts known to others. Third, language helps in the organization of thought. Fourth, language aids the development of creative ideas.

[1] Chukovsky, Kornei. *From Two to Five*, Berkeley, University of California Press, 1965, p. 24.

Language arts experiences for preschool children are concerned with more than the teaching of reading.

An authority in the field of language arts confirms this. "Surely, you can teach most four and five year olds to answer in long sentences and can even teach some of them to read. The question is, 'does this assure a reading, comprehending, thinking and questioning and communicating person, capable of socially meaningful action?' The answer is, 'not necessarily.'"[2] There is a definite difference between the ability to learn to read and the desire to do so. The growth and development of cognitive skills is much like learning about yourself-both are continuous processes. So it is with learning to read.

Before turning to the specific activities in acquiring speaking, listening, reading and writing skills, ask yourselves the following questions:

> Do I really listen to what the children are saying? There is little reason for children to speak clearly and distinctly if no one listens.

> Is there really a two way communication between the children and myself, or is it a monologue on my part?

> Do I involve the children in activities that lend themselves easily to verbal interaction, for example: cooking, puppetry, dramatic play, story telling, trip taking?

> Is the verbal interaction relevant to children's play or too abstract for them to comprehend?

> Does the interaction take place in the interest of mutual trust and respect; a mutual trust and respect based on the teacher's genuine friendliness, unconditional acceptance, warmth, empathy and interest?[3]

Positive answers to these questions contribute to making language exciting and worthwhile, and motivates children to acquire communication competency.

---

[2] Mattick, Ilse. "The Teacher's Role in Helping Children Develop Language Competence," *Young Children,* Volume XXVII, No. 3, Feb. 1972, p. 134.

[3] *Ibid.,* p. 142.

Speaking

In order for children to express ideas about things around them, they must first communicate about themselves.

Ideas That Encourage Speaking

V.I.P. OF THE WEEK BULLETIN BOARD

Design a bulletin board which is reserved for display by one child per week. Place pictures on the bulletin board that the child has brought in and talk   about them with the group. Also, display pictures which he has done in school or anything else which he wishes to exhibit. Finally, include any stories or poems that he has dictated to the teacher or another adult.

BODY TRACING

There is no better way of encouraging a child to speak about himself than with a body tracing. Body tracings are usually done on large pieces of Kraft brown paper. The child lies on the paper while another child or an adult traces around him. Once the outline is made, the child is free to decorate his tracing as he pleases including dressing himself with pieces of scrap material, putting hair on with yarn. An adult asks the child to tell a little about himself and his family as the child is working.

This activity is effectively done at the beginning of the school year. It provides an insight into the child's family life which is helpful to the teacher. Body painting is also a great deal of fun if the teacher is relaxed enough to let the chidren paint themselves. It is a marvelous activity for a hot summer day when done outside in front of a large mirror.

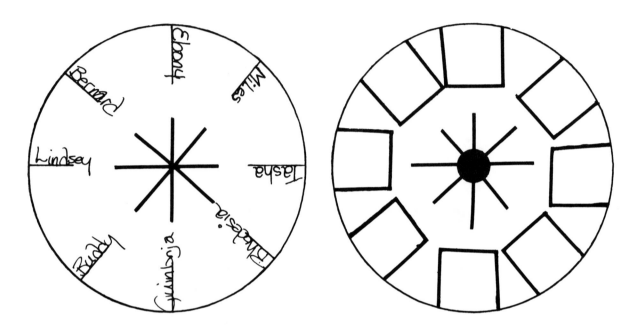

CLASSROOM PICTURE WHEEL
Pictures of each child are pasted on a wheel. Children's names are pasted on another wheel. Children match the picture with the name and tell a little about each other.

LITERATURE
Picture books including the *Family of Man, Children and their Mothers, Children and their Fathers, The Child* and other provocative pictures found in magazines are aids in discussions about self and family.

GROUP DISCUSSIONS ABOUT SELF, FEAR, EMOTIONS
Group discussions about self, fear and emotions may arise from events such as the death of a pet or family member. Group discussion alleviates anxiety, confusion and misinformation.

SPOKEN POETRY – CHORAL SPEAKING
Spoken poetry is fun for children at anytime. A few examples are as follows:

The Little Turtle

There was a little turtle
He lived in a box
He swam in a puddle, he climbed on the rocks,
He snapped at a mosquito, he snapped at a flea
He snapped at a minnow and he snapped at me.
He caught the mosquito and he caught the flea
He caught the minnow, BUT HE DIDN'T CATCH ME.

My Tongue

My tongue comes out on THIS and THAT
on THOSE and THESE and THEM.
It pops out too on THINK and THANK
But not on SIT and SAT.

Your Voice

Your outdoor voice is fine, I'd say
For shouting out of doors at play.
But in the house we would all rejoice
If you could use your indoor voice.

Your outdoor voice is big and gruff
And loudest when the games are rough.
Your indoor voice is soft and low
When you are indoors, please keep it so.

a time for words

The Wiggly Tooth
Once I had a wiggly tooth
It wobbled everyday
When I ate and when I drank
It wobbled every way.
Then I had some candy
A sticky taffy roll
And where my wiggly tooth had been
There's nothing but a hole!

When I talk to a Monkey
When you talk to a monkey
He seems very wise
He scratches his head
He blinks both eyes
But he won't say a word
He just sits on a rail
And makes a big question mark
Out of his tail.

STORY TELLING AND DRAMATIC PLAY

Story telling and dramatic play are probably as old as man's power of speech and are a most effective tool for communication today. Good story telling includes all aspects of experience and uses all facets of imagination and creativity. Stories should have a good plot with something of interest to resolve. Plots which have repetition, conflict and an uninterrupted main theme keep children's attention. Interest is further maintained if the story has some frame of reference for the listener. Don't forget the Hans Christian Anderson stories and the Grimm's Fairy Tales, as they are still favorites of children today.

Encourage children to make up their own stories and act them out in small groups. Even the smallest of children create stories which can be recorded, read and played back to the group, demonstrating that the spoken and written word has particular meaning to individual children as well as to a group.

LANGUAGE EXPERIENCES WITH BLOCKS

Egocentric children of two and three do not hold extended conversations with other children. Blocks provide a social outlet by which children gradually move from solitary play to parallel play situations with other children at ages 4-5. As interest in seeing what the other children are doing increases, verbal communication increases. The gas station which Billy is building is getting very large. Tasha brings in her truck and Sonja begins to build a garage next door. The children are moving into a cooperative play experience. Two garages are built and a road is made in front of the two.

Adults facilitate this social play experience by writing down the short conversations between builders to be read to them later, by taking dictation about the structures being built, and by photographing the finished products for later display.

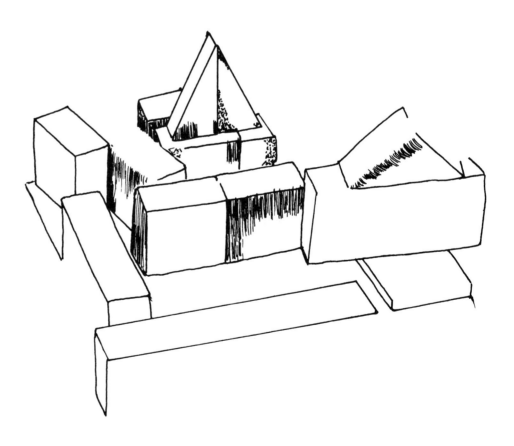

Listening

Children are aware of sounds early in their development. They respond differently to the sounds they hear. Two basics of sound — rhythm and tone — become an integral part of their thought process. They are actually the sign and symbol of thought. One of the best rhythmical tools in developing listening skills is repetition. Repetition represents variations based on a theme. Children gain self confidence and mastery of the language through repetition. Examples of books that offer rhythmic patterns are as follows:

Five Chinese Brothers — Claire Bishop
Three Billy Goats Gruff — Marcia Brown
The House that Jack Built — Randolph Caldecott
The Carrot Seed — Ruth Krauss
Caps for Sale — Esphyr Slobodkina
Goodnight Moon — Margaret Wise Brown
Green Eggs and Ham — Dr. Seuss
Mommy, Buy Me a China Doll — Harve and Margot Zemach
Do Baby Bears Sit in Chairs? — Ethel and Leonard Kessler
Where the Wild Things Are — Maurice Sendak

A more complete listing of popular children's books is found at the end of this section.

POETRY

Poetry is an excellent way to introduce rhythm. Arbuthnot's *A Time for Poetry,* published by Scott Foresman, is a classic in this field.

A young child comes to school essentially poetic. He is fascinated with the rhythmic qualities of the words around him. He trusts his senses and his sensory experiences. He finds much delight in the spoken word and playing with words. Poets such as Robert Frost, Edna St. Vincent Millay, Emily Dickenson, Carl Sandburg are classics.

Things to keep in mind when reading poetry with young children:
Poems should be at the interest level of most of the children.

Introduce a poem by asking a question related to the poem or by telling the children what the poem is about.

Movements are helpful in poetry to keep the interest of the children and to relax the body.

Inflection and tone are an important part and tool in the reading and understanding of a poem.

Children like poems about pets, play, children, their natural world, seasons, weather, animals, humor, make believe and that which is rich in sensory images and creation of mood.

Read poems that are appropriate to the season or capture the immediacy of an event which is happening in the classroom.

GAMES THAT AID DEVELOPMENT OF LISTENING SKILLS

Use hand clapping. Leader claps rhythms and the children tell the leader how many times they heard the clap. They then become the leader and clap a rhythm for the rest of the group.

Clap the rhythm of your name. Ex: Mrs. Johnson. Then clap a child's name. Ex: Peter Mahoney. The first time that you are doing this say the name of the child before clapping his name. Later clap a name and have the children guess whose name you are clapping.

Switch from clapping to the use of instruments — tone blocks, drums, rhythm sticks, are all excellent for this. Tap out familiar songs for the children to guess.

TAPE RECORDING

Recording is an exciting activity for children as well as adults. Have a tape recorder available for use by the children. Get them used to hearing their own voices and the voices of the other children and adults around them. Can they recognize the voices of others? Can they recognize their own voices? Do different tones in voices indicate different things to them?

Reading

Wouldn't it be delightful if there was one method of reading that a teacher could employ with equal success for every child that she teaches? Unfortunately, this is not the case, nor has there ever existed one standard method of teaching reading. There are many reasons why this is true, one being that there is no way of determining which method of reading is best in a given situation. The effectiveness of the method depends on the skill of the teacher with the different children, the backgrounds of the different children and how creatively she executes her skills.

Whichever method of teaching reading is used, it is important to keep in mind that anyone of the methods listed below can be successful. None guarantees success but all can be taught creatively. The following is a brief synopsis of a few different approaches used in teaching reading:

THE BASAL APPROACH

This developmental guided approach is a series of basal readers used progressively through the grades building vocabulary as they go. Materials are carefully systematized using workbooks, tests, and reading aids with each grade. Vocabulary is controlled and lesson plans are explained in a teacher's manual. Some basal reading features sight vocabulary. Others concentrate on phonics, still others focus on sound-symbol approach in so called linguistics.

The sight method concentrates on repetition and rote memory of words. Skills for decoding are not used until much later. The phonics method makes associations between sound of language and the way sounds are symbolized in print. Meaning is gained only after letter sound associations have been made. Linguistics encourages the recognition of patterns in words — Example: bat, that, fat, hat, etc. Gradually small but important differences are introduced — Example: hat, hit.

TOTAL COMMUNICATION (LANGUAGE EXPERIENCE)

Here the emphasis is on the child's own language and experiences. Though there are now some professionally prepared readers, the children create their own materials for the most part as they tell stories and dictate experiences for themselves and others to read. Reading here becomes part of the total communication process of listening, speaking, reading and writing. Skills are introduced incidentally, as the need arises. It is the meaning of words which is the most important.

INDIVIDUALIZED READING

This method encourages the child to follow his own interest in reading material. Skills are taught individually as the children need them and through many conferences with the teacher.

INDEPENDENT READING

Children learn through individual programmed instruction. This is often through a teaching machine. The child paces himself here and can usually correct his own mistakes as he goes along. Teachers are free to help the children who are having difficulty.

SYMBOLS

I.T.A. — Initial Teaching Alphabet or 44 symbols approach originated in England. This provides 44 symbols instead of 26, one for every sound in our language. Children learn to read by this method and then make the transition to the regular alphabet.

The following activities facilitate the teaching of reading with pre-school children who indicate an interest in learning to read. They are best used selectively and with small groups of children at one time.

WORD PICTURE DOMINOES

If children are capable of drawing their own pictures, this can successfully be incorporated into the learning process and experience. This activity assists children to learn initial consonants by increasing picture/word vocabulary. First, children see the word, then say it. A game is played by matching pictures to words as in regular dominoes.

Writing

INDIVIDUAL DICTIONARIES

On oak tag cards, 4" x 8½", children tell you the words that they are interested in spelling. Write out the word for them on a card. They then copy what you have written on their card and draw an appropriate picture.

> The words become important because they have meaning to the individual children who select them.
> The word is remembered because of the picture the child has associated with it.
> The child sees his spoken word in print.

WORDS AS PICTURES

Draw diagrams of words as they look by the shapes of the letters. Create a guessing game to recognize the word. Success is enhanced if exercise is first done on an experience chart with a small group.

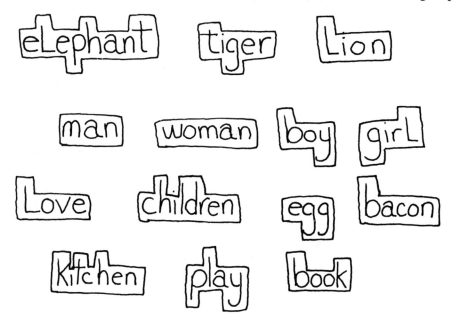

NAME AND WORD RECOGNITION

Design cards with the children's names on them. Place a shape next to the name. Corresponding shapes are in other parts of the room such as the cubbies. Children recognize their own names by matching names to corresponding shapes and colors.

LEARNING LETTER NAMES

This sense approach is used in learning the letter "M".

Taste: Distribute one M&M candy to each child. Look at the printed M on the candy. Child describes taste of M candy as he eats it.

Feeling: How does the letter M feel on your lips. Create an M box with different objects that begin with the letter M. Close your eyes and identify the objects.

Hearing: How does the letter M sound? Children go mmm mmmm mm mm m, listen to others, and then make the sound themselves.

Sight: The letter M has a special look. Describe the M. Record observations. Experiment writing the letter. Make a picture around the letter M hiding it in the picture so that you cannot see it in the picture. Following are descriptions that have been given about the letter M.

M has three points.

M has four lines.

M looks like a house if you break it in half.

M doesn't have windows or doors.

M looks like E on its side

M looks like cat's ears.

Small m looks like two toes.

Small m looks like an upside down w.

Small m looks like two bridges put together.

Create stories about M. Make M with your body.

THE WHEEL OF FORTUNE

Place two circles one smaller than the other on top of one another. Wheels should be loosely fastened so that they can move independently of one another. Initial consonants are printed on one side of the wheels and phonograms "ar, am, at" are printed around the other wheel. By rotation, different words are formed.

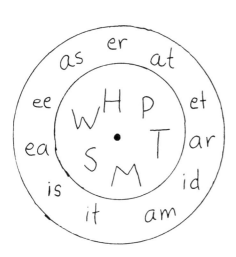

BOOK BINDING

Materials   Turpentine   Elmers Glue
              Oil paints   Scissors
              Tray or pan   Construction paper
              Plain paper   Needle
              Plastic tape   Thread
              Cardboard

Procedure   Mix oil paint with a little turpentine and stir well. Put all toge-
              ther in a tray or pan. Add one tablespoon of paint mixture to
              water. The paint will float. Drop a sheet of paper into the water
              and paint mixture and leave for a few seconds. Lay the paper on
              the table to dry. (At least 30 minutes.)

              To prepare the cover, lay 2 pieces of cardboard of equal size
              next to one another. They should be 1/8 of an inch apart.
              Cover the 1/8" space with plastic tape 1-1/8" wide, sticky
              side facing up. Fold the excess tape over the top and bottom of
              the cardboard.

              Put glue on the back of the construction paper and glue it to the
              cover. Smooth out the excess glue and let it dry.

              This is an extended activity for older preschool children. It
              takes a few days to complete. Once completed, however, the
              books become an integral part of the preschool experience and
              may be a place to record all the events of the day in picture
              and word form.

              Choose a painted cover to match the tape. Fold paper in half
              and cut along the fold. Cover the back side of the paper with
              glue. Line the paper up with the tape and smooth it over the
              cardboard. Cut off the corners and fold them over the card-
              board. Set it off to dry.

              Take sheets of unlined paper and fold them in half. Match
              two pieces of construction paper to the size of the unlined
              paper. This paper should be ¼" smaller than the cover. Crease
              the paper in the middle. Thread a large eyed needle with heavy
              thread. Do not knot the thread. The thread should be three
              times the length of the book. Poke five holes through the crease
              of the book. Beginning in the middle, sew from the middle hole
              to the outside until all the holes have been joined. End in the
              middle and tie a knot.

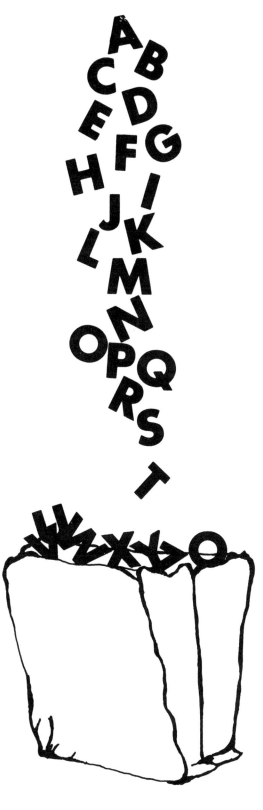

DISCRIMINATION AND RECOGNITION

AUDITORY DISCRIMINATION

Sound Effects: Tell a story as children make the sound effects.

Telling Sounds: Eyes closed, the players are asked to tell what it is that is making the particular sound.

Clap: Players clap when the word that is said does not begin with the same letter as the other ones in a group.

Guess the Word: Tell a story and leave out a word but tell the beginning sound. The players have to guess which word is missing.

AUDITORY RECOGNITION

Seeing Sounds: Players discover words that begin with the same sound as the words that are pronounced.

Games:

Games develop particular skills. Below are some to be played by pre-school children involving activities in Visual and Auditory recognition.

LETTER DISCRIMINATION

The Letter Ladder
Place a letter card at the bottom rung of a ladder. Throw other letter cards on the floor. Children match the letter on the floor with the letter on the ladder, inserting the correct one as they go.

The Word Basket
Keep a word basket in the corner of the room. Match words that begin alike and end alike.

Find a Twin
Find the word in the basket that is exactly like the one that the leader is holding up.

Scramble
There are two ladders. Some words are placed on one ladder and others on the other ladder. Players are asked to straighten out the two ladders so that they match.

VISUAL RECOGNITION

Bingo
Place colored paper over letters on a bingo card as they are called and matched. The first one to have covered all the letters on the card wins.

Pick Up
Words are dropped on the floor. The players pick up all the ones that can be recognized.

Circle Game
Circle all the words or letters on a sheet of paper that are the same.

Post Office
One child is the postmaster. Words are written on envelopes. Players that can recognize the words get the letters.

Selected References

Language Development

Arbuthnot, Mary Hill. *Children and Books.* Revised Edition. Chicago: Scott Foresman & Co., 1964.

——————, *A Time for Poetry.* Glenview, Illinois: Scott Foresman and Co., 1968.

Chukovsky, Kornei. *From Two to Five.* Berkeley: University of California Press, 1963.

Dale, Philips. *Language Development: Structure and Function.* Hinsdale, Illinois: Dryden Press, 1972.

Durkin, Dolores. *Teaching Young Children to Read.* Boston: Allyn and Bacon, 1972.

Hirsch, Elizabeth S., ed. *The Block Book.* Washington, D.C.: National Association for the Education of Young Children, 1974.

Mattick, Ilse. The teachers role in helping young children develop language competence. *Young Children,* 1972, Volume XXVII, No. 3, 134-142.

McCarthy, D. Language development in children. In, L. Carmichael (ed.) *Manual of Child Psychology.* New York: Wiley, 1954.

Piaget, Jean. *The Language and Thought of the Child.* New York: World, 1955.

Rainey, Ernestine. *Language Development in the Young Child.* Atlanta, Ga.: Humanics Press. 1976.

Rosen, Connie and Harold. *The Language of Primary School Children.* Baltimore, Md.: Penguin Books, 1973.

Sandberg, John H., Pohlman, Joanne D. Reading on the child's terms. *Young Children,* 1976, Volume XXXI, No. 2, 106-112.

Steichen, Edward. *The Family of Man.* New York: Maco Magazine Corporation. 1955.

Vygotsky, Lev. S. *Thought and Language.* Cambridge, Mass.: M.I.T. Press, 1962.

Winsor, Charlotte B. *Dimensions of Language Experience.* New York: Agathon Press, 1975.

A Brief Selection of Children's Favorite Books

Bemelmans, Ludwig. *Madeline.* Illustrated by the Author. New York: Viking Press, 1939.

——————, *Madeline and the Bad Hat.* Illustrated by the Author. New York: Viking Press, 1957.

——————, *Madeline and the Gypsies.* Illustrated by the Author. New York: Viking Press. 1973.

——————, *Madeline's Rescue.* Illustrated by the Author. New York: Viking Press, 1973.

Birnbaum, A. *Green Eyes.* Illustrated by the Author. Western Publisher, 1973.

Bishop, Claire H; & Wise, Kurt. *Five Chinese Brothers.* New York: Coward McCann Inc., 1938.

Brown, Marcia. *Stone Soup.* Illustrated by the Author. N. J. 1947.

——————, *Three Billy Goats Gruff.* Illustrated by the Author. New York: Harcourt Brace, 1957.

Brown, Margaret Wise. *City Noisy Book.* Illustrated by Leonard Weisgard. Pennsylvania: Harper and Row, 1939.

——————, *Country Noisy Book.* Illustrated by Leonard Weisgard. Pennsylvania: Harper and Row, 1940.

——————, *The Dead Bird.* Mass.: Addison-Wesley, 1958.

——————, *Goodnight Moon.* Illustrated by Clement Hurd. Pennsylvania: Harper and Row, 1947.

Burton, Virginia Lee. *The Little House.* New York: Houghton Mifflin, 1942.

——————, *Mike Mulligan and his Steam Shovel.* New York: Houghton Mifflin Co.

Dr. Seuss. *Five Hundred Hats of Bartholomew Cubbins.* New York: Vanguard.

——————, Illustrated by the Author. *Green Eggs and Ham.* New York: Vanguard, 1960.

——————, Illustrated by the Author. *Horton Hears A Who.* New York: Random House, 1954.

Caldecott, Randolph. *The House That Jack Built.* Illustrated by the Author. New York: Watts, 1967.

DeRegniers, Beatrice Schenk. *May I Bring a Friend?* New York: Atheneum, 1964.

Ets, Marie Hall. *Gilberto and the Wind.* New York: Viking Press, 1963.

Fassler, Joan. *My Grandpa Died Today.* Illustrated by Stuard Kranz. New York: Behavioral Publication Inc., 1971.

Freeman, Donald. *Corduroy.* New York: Viking, 1968.

Gag, Wanda. *Millions of Cats.* New York: Coward McCann, 1938.

——————, *More Tales from Grimm.* New York: Coward McCann, Inc., 1947.

——————, *Nothing at All.* New York: Coward McCann, Inc., 1941.

——————, *Tales from Grimm.* New York: Coward McCann, Inc., 1936.

Hazen, Barbara Shook. Illustrated by Leigh Grant. *Why Couldn't I Be an Only Kid Like You, Wigger?* New York: Atheneum, 1975.

Keats, Ezra Jack. *Letter to Amy.* Illustrated by the Author. Pa.: Harper and Row, 1968.

——————, *Peter's Chair.* Illustrated by the Author. Pa.: Harper and Row, 1967.

——————, *Snowy Day.* Illustrated by the Author. New York: Viking Press, 1962.

——————, *Whistle for Willie.* Illustrated by the Author. New York: Viking Press, 1969.

Krauss, Ruth. *Birthday Party.* Illustrated by Maurice Sendak. Pa.: Harper and Row, 1957.

——————, *Carrot Seed.* Illustrated by J. Crocket. Pa.: Harper and Row, 1945.

——————, *A Hole is to Dig: A first book of definitions.* Illustrated by Maurice Sendak. Pa.: Harper and Row, 1952.

——————, *A Very Special House.* Illustrated by Maurice Sendak, Pa.: Harper and Row, 1953.

Kessler. Ethel & Leonard. *Do Baby Bears Sit in Chairs?* New York, Doubleday.

Lapsley, Susan. Illustrated by Michael Charlton. *I Am Adopted.* Scarsdale, N. Y.: Bradbury Press, 1975.

Lionni, Leo. *Fish is Fish.* Illustrated by the Author. Maryland: Pantheon, 1974.

—————, *Frederick.* Illustrated by the Author. Maryland: Pantheon, 1966.

—————, *Inch by Inch.* Illustrated by the Author. New York: Astor Honor, 1962.

—————, *Little Blue and Little Yellow.* New York: Astor and Honor, 1959.

McClosky, Robert. *Blueberries for Sal.* New York: Viking Press, 1969.

—————, *Make Way for Ducklings.* New York: Viking Press, 1969.

Munari, Bruno. *Circus in the Mist.* New York: World, 1968.

Ness, Evaline. *Sam Bangs and Moonshine.* New York: Holt, Reinhard and Winston, 1966.

Potter, Beatrix. *The Tale of Peter Rabbit.* Michigan: Fideler Co., 1946.

Reed, Philip. *Mother Goose and Nursery Rhymes.* New York: Atheneum, 1963.

Rey, Margaret. *Curious George Goes to the Hospital.* Boston: Houghton Mifflin, 1966.

Rockwell, Anne. *Three Bears and Fifteen Other Stories.* New York: Thomas Y. Crowell, 1975.

Rockwell, Harlow. *My Dentist.* Illustrated by the Author. New York: Greenwillow Books, 1975.

Slobodkina, Esphyr. *Caps for Sale.* New York: William R. Scott, 1947.

Sendak, Maurice. *Chicken Soup with Rice.* A Book of the Month. Illustrated by the Author. School Book Service. 1970.

—————, *In the Night Kitchen.* Illustrated by the Author. Pa.: Harper and Row, 1970.

—————, *Let's Be Enemies.* New York: Harper and Row, 1970.

—————, *Where the Wild Things Are.* Pa.: Harper and Row, 1963.

Smith, Grace. Graphics by Margi Schultz Design. *The Hospital is Where.* California: 1417 Ocean Dr., 1975.

Wildsmith, Brian. *Brian Wildsmith's ABC's.* Illustrated by the Author, New York: Watts, 1963.

—————, *Brian Wildsmith's Birds.* Illustrated by the Author, New York: Watts, 1967.

—————, *Brian Wildsmith's Circus.* Illustrated by the Author. New York: Watts, 1970.

—————, *Brian Wildsmith's Wild Animals.* Illustrated by the Author. New York: Watts, 1967.

Zemach, Harve and Margot. *Mommy, Buy Me a China Doll.* New York: Farrar, Strauss and Giroux, Inc., 1975.

Zolotow, Charlotte. *If It Weren't For You.* Illustrated by Ben Shector. New York: Harper and Row, 1966.

—————, *The Quareling Book.* Illustrated by Arnold Lobel. New York: Harper and Row, 1963.

—————, *A Father Like That.* New York: Harper and Row, 1971.

—————, *Big Brother.* New York: Harper and Row, 1960.

—————, *William's Doll.* New York: Harper and Row, 1972.

part 6 / ask the wizard

Introduction
The Senses
Electricity
Magnetism
Living Things
Measurement and Volume
Selected References

Introduction

The emphasis of science instruction in the past has been on the 'what' of science, the products of the scientist. There has not been enough concern in the 'how' of science, the process of science. Significantly, however, it is the process activities that are realistic and appropriate for young children, not the factual content material.

Donald Neuman

The goal of this chapter of *Child's Play* is to provide material that will expose children to scientific exploration;

> to sharpen children's observation of the world around them;
> to help children recognize similarities and differences;
> to make comparisons;
> to develop the ability to make judgments and predictions accurately.

Observations are based on use of the five senses; sight, smell, taste, sound and touch. Sorting, mentioned in the chapter on mathematics, is also a scientific concept. We sort things on the basis of the similar properties. Which group has all the blues? Who has all the wooden blocks? Put all the folating materials in one pile.

Science activities for young children are important for a number of reasons. They promote cognitive growth allowing children to

---

[1] Neuman, Donald. "Sciencing for Young Children" *Young Children;* Volume XXVII, No. 4, April, 1972, p. 215.

develop abstract concepts from the concrete activities. A gallon of water is still a gallon of water whether it is in a tall skinny container or a fat wide one. Science activities increase vocabulary and help children distinguish relative size, shape, similarities and differences. Science activities aid in small muscle development. The screwing of a wire onto a terminal of a battery requires manual dexterity. Finally, as children increase their scientific skills and sharpen techniques of inquiry, they develop an ability to make accurate predictions

Science activities take place out doors as well as indoors. Every outdoor adventure can be turned into a potential science experience. This includes anything from finding a bird's nest to watching lightening and listening to thunder on a rainy day. These activities spark discussion leading to creative writing and art.

Child's Play: An Activities and Materials Handbook

The Senses

SIGHT

Purpose   To develop keen observation skills.

Color Dilution Trays

Materials   Food color
Water —different bases, i.e., oil
Square ice cube trays or chemical dilution trays
Eye droppers

Procedure   Fill the trays with water. Place one drop of food coloring in one corner and another drop in the diagonal corner. Give children an eyedropper to experiment with different mixtures of color. Do not draw up all of the color on the first squeeze of the dropper. If you do the variety of color will be limited.

Mixing Paints

Materials   Primary colors (red, blue, yellow, white)
Pint size plastic ice cream containers

Procedure   Begin by mixing two colors to create a third:
         Red + Yellow = Orange
         Red + Blue = Purple
         Blue + Yellow = Green
         Red + Blue + Yellow = Brown

As the children watch you do this, they will become skilled enough to mix small quantities on their own. Put two colors out on the table with a can of water. Mix colors in varying degrees to get new shades of color. Next, cut out all the colors that have been created and paste them onto a large sheet of paper. Name the colors that they have produced. Some results of this have been:

     "Sunshine Orange from red + yellow
     "Peppermint Red" from red + white
     "Grassy Green" from green + white
     "Midnight Blue" from blue and black
     "Prince Purple" from blue and red
See *Awareness of the Arts* for further art activities.

Displaying Objects

Materials   Sea shells, rocks, natural materials, various bones, leaves, wood, plants.
Microscope
Magnifying glass

Procedure   Place objects on the table. Prepare questions about each object. Example: Can you find all the things which come from the sea? All of the observations that are made are recorded in a book which is left in the science area at all times.

Melting

Materials   Ice
Ice shavings
Snow
Icicles

Procedure   Place frozen materials into containers. How quickly do they melt? Ask questions like: Which frozen material melted the fastest? Why? What can we do to make these frozen things last longer? What can we do to speed up the process?

SMELL

Purpose   To distinguish different smells.

Materials   Flowers, plants, common household products, spices, pine, hay, mint, common foods (onions, etc.) vinegar, nail polish remover, water.

Procedure   Describe how the different items smell. How are they similar? Different? Do they effect any other senses? (Onions make your eyes water.)

Exploring the outside through smell:

Go for a walk. Do the grass and the trees have a different smell? Do certain smells remind you of different things? (Hay = Barn) What does wet wood smell like?

TOUCH

Purpose   To develop a discriminating sense of touch.

Materials   Gather all kinds of cloth materials (rough and smooth), various kinds of wood, different grades of sand paper, etc.

Procedure   The object of this project is to increase children's awareness of the different ways common materials feel. Encourage children to collect different textured items outside and indoors. Record their observations.

Make a Feel Box:

Materials   A box that is closed but that has an opening just large enough for a child's hand.
Various objects that will fit into the box.

Procedure   Place objects into the box. Without looking, ask children to identify these objects one at a time. Place similar objects on a tray. Children match these objects with those in the box.

Feel the Wind

Take the children outside and ask them to feel the wind blowing on their face — watch what the wind does to your hair and clothes. Look at different things blowing — flags, smoke, leaves. Name differences in wind: brisk, gentle, hurricane, etc.

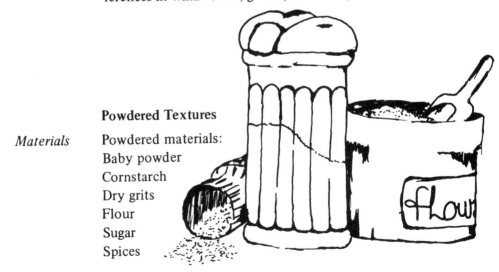

Powdered Textures

Materials   Powdered materials:
Baby powder
Cornstarch
Dry grits
Flour
Sugar
Spices

Procedure   Children feel powders explaining differences in texture such as soft, rough. Which feel the same? Which feel different?

TASTE

Purpose   To identify various substances on the basis of taste.

Materials   Various common liquids and spices such as:
        Lemon juice
        Tea
        Sugar, salt, flour
        Orange juice

Procedure   The children see the items first and then are blind-folded as they identify familiar tastes. (Note: There is an extensive recipe list in the following section which serves as a basis for initial cooking experiences with children.)

SOUND

Sounds are all around us, ranging from a ticking clock to a blaring car horn — dogs barking, rain falling, leaves rustling. Sounds occur through vibrations. You can feel these vibrations in a guitar string, on a radio or a piano string.

Purpose   To increase awareness of everyday sounds.

Hearing Music Sound as it Moves:

Materials   Glass of water
Tuning fork

Procedure   Strike a tuning fork on a rubber heel and hold one of the prongs against the water. Observe the splashing and listen to the sound.

Watching vibrations:

Material   Ruler
Table

Procedure   Place a ruler on a table with most of it projecting beyond the table's edge. Hold the part on the ruler firmly against the table with one hand. Press down lightly on the free end and let the ruler snap back. Watch it vibrate and listen for a musical sound. Move the ruler back on the table with less of it projecting. How does the note change?

Simple Instruments:

You can make simple one string instruments and experiment with changing pitch by shortening and lengthening the string. (See The Song is Love)

Materials   Piece of wood (1'x1'x¼") Triangular block. Fishing line.

Procedure   Take the long piece of wood and in the middle of each end make a saw cut ¼" deep. Two inches from one end, glue the triangular block to make a bridge. Take a 14" piece of monofilament fishing line and insert each end in a brass paper fastener. Coil the next one inch or so around the fastener and put the fastener over the underside. Children can then experiment with changing the length of the string and noticing the change in the pitch of the note.

Materials   Coffee cans
Beans
Rocks
Coins

Procedure   Fill the coffee cans with varied amounts of coins, rocks or beans. Shake the cans listening for differences in sound. Does the difference in amount and kind of material alter the sound? Experiment with containers of other materials — plastic, paper, etc. What does that do to the sound?

Materials   Glasses
Water
Soft drink bottles

Procedure   Fill the glasses with varying levels of water and tap them with a piece of metal. Does the sound vary with the different amount of water? Does the size of the glass make a difference in the sound? Do the same thing with soft drink bottles and blow into them. What does the amount of liquid have to do with the sound?

Simple Banjos

Materials   Rubber bands
Milk cartons

Procedure   Cut a rectangle from the side of a milk carton, leaving a ¼" margin all around. Thumbtack a wooden brace across the opening and put 8 rubber bands around the carton equally spaced. Tighten or loosen each of the strings by pulling on them. Experiment with thicker or thinner rubber bands.

Electricity

ELECTRIC CHARGES

On a cold, dry clear day, wearing leather soled shoes, scuff across a woolen rug and then gently touch a metal plate. What do you see, hear, feel?

Try this again in a darkened room. Place several different objects on a table — a needle, a penny, a large nail, a metal baking pan, a piece of paper, a book. Which of these give shocks? Which don't?

Run a comb briskly through your hair. Is the hair attracted to the comb after you do this? Does the experiement work as well with a comb that has not been used?

CURRENT ELECTRICITY

Vocabulary:

Insulators — materials which hinder the flow of electricity: Ex: rubber, plastic, cloth, paper.
Conductors — materials which provide an easy path for electricity: Ex: a penny, tin foil, knife blade.
Circuit — the path which electricity follows. If electricity follows a complete path back to the beginning, the circuit is closed. If the electricity is prevented from making a complete path, the circuit is open.
Direct Charge — d.c.— electrons moving in one direction through a dry cell.

Alternating Current — a.c. — current not supplied from a cell or battery — not a one direction current.

Series circuit — cells arranged in such a way that the voltage of one is added to that of the next by a wire connection.

Parallel Circuits — these are connected in such a way to give longer power not double strength. Each cell works only a fraction of its real strength.

EXPERIMENTS WITH ELECTRICITY : Completing a Circuit.

Materials

One ½ volt dry cell battery
Copper wire
Small electric bulbs

Procedure

Unscrew the nuts at the top of the battery. Wind the wire around the top of one of the terminals and connect it to the base of a bulb. Wind another wire around the other terminal and connect it to same bulb. The bulb should light.

Magnetism

WHAT DO MAGNETS ATTRACT?

Materials

Magnets	Pennies
Paperclips	Pieces of wood, etc.
Hairpins	

Procedure

Find all the different things that magnets attract. Record observations and draw conclusions. What items do magnets attract? Try chalk, money, nails, buttons.

MAGNETS HAVE POLES

Materials

Bar magnets
Tacks
Paper brads

Procedure

Lay a strong bar magnet on a piece of paper which you have sprinkled with tacks and wire brads. Notice where the pieces cluster. The places that are usually the strongest are the ends, or poles of the magnet. Notice that there is a north pole marked N and a south pole marked S.

Test what happens when you put two similar poles together.

What happens when you put opposite poles together.

Place a magnet under a piece of white paper. Sprinkle the paper with iron filings. Notice the magnetism around the poles. What does the tapping of the paper do? Does the magnetism occur in straight lines or curves?

ELECTROMAGNETS

Materials   1½ volt dry cell battery
Covered copper wire
Large nails
Metal objects
Paper objects
Wood objects

Procedure   Wrap the wire in a coil effect around the nail. Connect one end of it to one terminal of the dry cell. Connect the other end to the other terminal. Test the nail to see what object it will pick up. What happens if you disconnect the wire?

Living Things

In exploring the environment, children come across many exciting living things, all of which are an integral part of any science program. Caring for plants and animals gives children responsibility in the classroom and an understanding of the life cycles of different living things.

Place plants and animals in various parts of the room instead of grouping them all together. Animals which are particularly adaptable to the classroom are rabbits, gerbils, guinea pigs, fish and hamsters. Take precautions so that things that do not belong in the fish tank do not get dropped in by accident. This is part of learning the responsibility for the care of living things in the room.

Plants are fun to observe and measure as they grow. They also provide aesthetic quality and give the room a homey, lived-in look. For that reason, scatter them around the room giving special attention to ivy, ferns, and other plants which do not require direct sunlight. Staged plants provide functional room dividers.

Specific planting activities go on all year long.

FALL PLANTING

Plant bulbs while the ground is still unfrozen (if you live in a cold climate) so that you will have spring flowers. This not only provides a fall activity, but also, it is something that you can remind the children of in the cold winter months.

FALL ART PROJECTS

Iron leaves between pieces of waxed paper.
Paint leaves and use them in collage.
Make a fall tree using real as well as cut out leaves.
Make a visit to a cider mill and watch the cider being pressed.
>   Make your own cider.
>   Have sliced apples for snack.
>   Create apple desserts.

TERRARIUM

Since planting is inappropriate during the winter months, in some climates, this is an ideal time for a terrarium. Any glass or plastic container can be used. Something must be added to the bottom to provide for adequate drainage. Sand and small gravel or stones are good. Charcoal prevents mildew from occurring. Plant a wood terrarium, or cacti, or ferns and moss. Keep out of direct sunlight and in a place that is not too warm.

Materials   Large mouth glass jar or wide plastic containers.

Procedure   Place some gravel and/or sand on the bottom. Dig up small plants being careful to dig around and under for topsoil. Include small animals, bugs, worms, etc. Add a little water to the soil and leaves. Seal the glass jar or tape another plastic container on the original one (small holes in the top will be needed). Place in direct sun. Water once a month.

SPRING AND SUMMER PLANTING

Planting during these seasons revolves around vegetables and flowers which can be started inside and moved out when the threat of frost disappears. *The Beginning Gardener* is a good source book for you to begin with. It is written by Katherine Cutter.

No science program would be complete without the use of the outdoors. Begin in the Fall by noticing the leaves changing color.

SPRING ACTIVITIES

For spring, gather cocoons, bird nests and set up a bird cage using natural branches from out of doors to fill the cage. The beauty of most indoor school cages is that they have a natural look instead of being made up of a lot of store bought materials. Try to keep things as simple as possible. Bird cages need be nothing more than a wood frame with a piece of plastic stretched around it with a mesh at the top for air. It can be any shape and size. Make sure that the cage has a door for easy cleaning. Parakeets, canaries, finches and parrots are suggested birds which can be found at local pet shops.

Don't forget collection of insects, ant farms, worm farms and fossil hunting.

WINTER WEATHER

In the Winter, observe changes in the weather.

> Colder winter days
> Possibility of snow
> Less hours of sunlight

Discuss how this weather effects the activities that the children do after school. How must they dress differently and what do they feel like when they come in from playing in the cold? These are good days for making hot snacks like soup or hot chocolate.

Make a weather calendar to chart the weather and discuss it daily.

Discuss how animals prepare for winter. Do humans go through the same process? What foods are special to the Fall and Winter? Discussion of harvesting is appropriate.

Out of doors can be fun in the winter. Make a snowman, snow angels, and observe melting and freezing. Experiment with a thermometer recording temperature and measurement of degrees.

Adapted from:
Rainey, Ernestine W. *Language Development for the Young Child: A Language Skill Workbook for Teaching Preschool Children.* Atlanta, Georgia: Humanics Press, 1976.

ask the wizard

Measurement and Volume

MEASURING VOLUME
(See the Chapter on Math for further activities.)
Water Play

Materials
Large area for water play
Different shaped plastic containers
Plastic tubing
Funnel
Spoons
Measuring cups

Procedure
Leave the materials out and available for the children to explore. Familiarize them with the different units of measure that they customarily see — a quart of milk, a pint of ice cream, etc.

Do they see the difference in size? How many pints does it take to fill up a quart container? Does a quart container always have to look the same to hold the same amount of liquid?

FLOATING AND SINKING

Gather different materials from around the room — cork, paper, wood, plastic, etc. Experiment to see which of the items will stay afloat. Make a list of those that do and those that do not. Make sailboats out of toothpicks, cork and paper sails.

DRY SAND
Liquid properties of sand
Observe the different ways children go about filling containers. Do they pour? Do they use their hands? Ask them questions such as: How many ways can you fill your container without using your hands? Will dry sand stream out of the same containers as water? Does sand flow through a tube?

Differences in Sand

All sand is not alike. Gravel is a form of sand. Does gravel do the same things as fine sands? If there are two kinds of sand, can they be separated? Make a sieve for the children that will allow the sand to go through but which holds the gravel.

Sand Pendulum

Materials   Tin can
Milk carton
Hammer and nails

Procedure   Make a hole in a tin can or milk carton by hammering a nail through the bottom. Hammer from the middle out and then cover the edges carefully without blocking the hole. The edges of the hole should not interfere with the sand passing out. Make three more holes at the top of the can. Suspend the pendulum over a sandbox, tray or shallow box. Fill it with sand and start moving it back and forth to make a picture.

You can make a permanent picture by putting glue on a piece of paper under the pendulum in a pattern and then swinging the pendulum. Add food coloring to the sand for a colored picture. Do different colors separately. Try drawing the pattern of movement the pendulum will take. Can it be controlled?

Some Dry Sand Materials

Possible containers:
Cardboard or wooden box at least 2 feet by 3 feet. Large pot or tube or packet.

Sand:
River or beach sand. Well dried oven baked. Coarse sand or gravel.

Equipment:
whole tins

Make sure before you give these containers to the children, the sand flows through the holes.

Funnels, troughs and tubes
Sieves or sifters
Wire mesh in a frame, wide tin with many holes in the bottom.

Selected References

Busch, Phyllis. *A Walk in the Snow.* New York: Lippincott, 1971.

Cutler, Katherine. *The Beginning Gardner.* New York: Barrows, 1961.

Eby, Carol; Kaup, Rachel; and Lader, Estelle. *Fostering Growth in Mathe-Matical Skills and Scientific Inquiry.* Darien, Conn.: Teachers Publishing Corporation, The Threshold Program for Early Learning, 1970.

Electricity and Magnetism. Ithica, New York: Cornell Science Leaflet, Volume 50, No. 3, 1957.

Epstein, Sam & Beryl. *Take This Hammer.* Illustrated by Tomie De Paulo. New York: Hawthorn, 1969.

Freeman, Mae & Ira. *The Story of Electricity.* New York: Random House, 1961.

————, *Your Wonderful World of Science.* New York: Random House, 1957.

Greene, Carla. *I Want to Be a Scientist.* Illustrated by J. La Salle. Chicago: Childrens, 1961.

Harlan, Jean Durgin. From curiosity to concepts: science experiences in the preschool. *Young Children,* 1975, Volume XXX, No. 4, 249-255.

————, *Science Experiences for the Early Childhood Years.* Columbus, Ohio: Charles E. Merrill, 1976.

McGrath, Thomas, & Jenkyns, Chris. *Beautiful Things.* New York: Vanguard, 1960.

Neuman, Donald. Sciencing for young children. *Young Children,* 1972, Volume XXVII, No. 4, 215-226.

Neumeyer, Peter F. *Why We Have Day and Night.* Mass.: Addison-Wesley, 1970.

Podendorf, Illa. *Discovering Science on Your Own.* Chicago: Childrens, 1962.

——————, *Living Things Change.* Chicago: Childrens, 1971.

——————, *The True Book of Science Experiments.* Chicago: Childrens, 1972.

Russell, Solveig P. *Like and Unlike: A First Look at Classification.* Illustrated by Lawrence DiFiori. New York: Walck, 1973.

Schneider, Herman & Nina. *How Big is Big?* Mass.: Addison-Wesley, 1946.

——————, *Science is Fun for You in a Minute or Two.* Illustrated by Leonard Kessler. New York: McGraw Hill Co., 1975.

——————, *Science is Fun with a Flashlight.* Illustrated by Harriet Sherman. New York: McGraw Hill Co., 1975.

——————, *Science Experiments in the Classroom.* Ithica, New York: Cornell Science Leaflet, Volume 55, No. 3, 1962.

Shaw, Peter. *Science: Informal Schools in Britain Today.* New York: Citation, 1972.

——————, *Sound.* Ithica, New York: Cornell Science Leaflet, Volume 54, No. 1, 1960.

part 7 / child's play cook book

Introduction
Breakfast and Healthy Baked Snacks
General Snacks
Fruit and Vegetable Treats
Party and Holiday Favorites

Introduction

Cooking has become a favorite activity in preschool programs in the past few years. Cooking is fun — it is a total experience, encompassing all other curriculum areas. *Child's Play* has emphasized that children learn best when they are in a flexible environment, when they are permitted to explore materials freely, when they engage in stimulating verbal interaction, and when they work with materials which sharpen their observation and prediction skills. What better place to develop these skills than through cooking. Preschool children are developing eating habits which will stay with them throughout their lives. A planned, nutritional cooking program will have far reaching implications for years to come.

Does this sound familiar to you? "I want to cook, but:
>   I don't have a kitchen.
>   I don't have a stove.
>   I have no money for cooking.
>   The children are not old enough, they will be hurt.
>   The children I work with can't read the recipes.
>   I can't cook with all 15 children at once."

Let's tackle these problems one at a time.

NO ACCESS TO A KITCHEN

Many child care programs do not have easy access to kitchen facilities. Two areas in the classroom can easily be converted into cooking space. These are the housekeeping and art areas. Criteria for selecting cooking space include:

An area with no carpeting

An area near running water

An uncluttered, protected, and easily accessible space.

NO AVAILABLE STOVE

Many recipes can be prepared without the use of a stove. If you prepare recipes which need heat, consider electric frying pans with large covers, mini-ovens, corn poppers, waffle irons or hot plates. Other utensils necessary for cooking include:

Mixing bowls of various sizes

Large spoons, preferably wooden with long handles

Small spoons, forks and knives

Measuring spoons

Plastic measuring cups

Air tight containers

Spatulas

Baking Pans of all sizes

Cookie sheets

Hot pads

Pot holders

Timers

Can openers

Clean up material

Extension cords

Storage materials such as wax paper, tin foil, plastic wrap and plastic bags.

NO BUDGET FOR COOKING

In some child care programs you may ask for and receive donations for cooking. This is done through parent groups, and local super markets. It is also possible to discuss the recipe that is being prepared a day before the cooking exercise. Send a note home with the children explaining what will be prepared the next day and assign each child an item to bring. This does two things. It gives the child a sense of responsibility for and contribution to the classroom activities, and it also gives him something to look forward to for the next group meeting.

SAFETY IN COOKING

First and foremost, choose activities which are appropriate for the age of the child with whom you work. Two and three year olds are good at tearing and, therefore, enjoy making salads, tearing lettuce and shelling beans. They also enjoy scooping whipped cream and mixing fruit salad. Fours and fives are capable of cutting food and preparing recipes that require heat, provided safety rules have been discussed with them.

First, discuss basic cleanliness such as washing hands before and after the cooking experience, not sticking fingers into mixture while it is being prepared, using clean utensils and cleaning up after the activity has been completed.

Second, when cooking over the stove or a hot plate, supply pot holders, turn pot handles away from the individual who is cooking, do not leave cloth and paper products near the heat and pay attention to cords on the floor, taping them down to prevent tripping.

Third, when cutting, choose utensils which are easy to handle. Short pairing knives are appropriate as are fruit scissors. Teach children the proper way of cutting away from themselves and monitor all cutting activities.

Fourth, provide child sized equipment in order to prevent falls caused by children standing on chairs and reaching for hot items on the stove.

Continue to discuss safety precautions before, throughout the cooking exercise and at its conclusion.

PREPARING EXPERIENCE CHARTS

An experience chart is a large piece of paper on which a recipe has been drawn using pictures as well as words. It can be prepared before the cooking experience and displayed while the cooking is going on, or it can be prepared with the children as part of the total cooking experience. Experience charts can be drawn, or created as a collage, using magazine pictures and actual cooking items. Each cooking experience should be accompanied by an experience chart. Children find them easy to follow and it encourages them to practice such prereading skills as sequencing, matching, and following directions.

Following is an example of a presentation of a cooking experience:

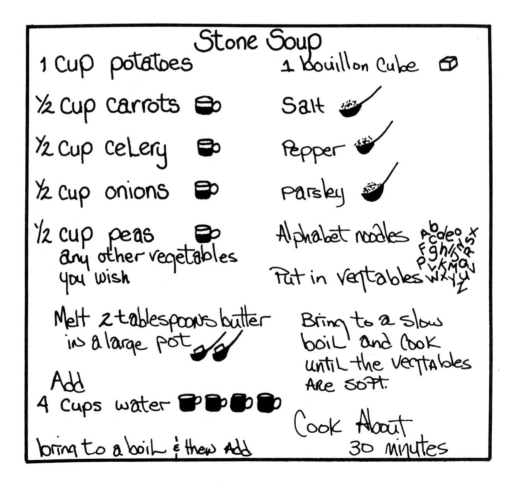

Child's Play: An Activities and Materials Handbook

PREPARATION OF STONE SOUP

One day before the preparation of Stone Soup, the book *Stone Soup* is read to the children. *(Stone Soup,* retold by Willis Lindquist, illustrated by Bob Shein.) This is the story of a boy who brings a hungry village together by making soup to which each person contributes some of what he has. The little boy starts by throwing a stone into the pot, as the first contribution, thereby encouraging each person to add just one vegetable to make it taste better. After the story of Stone Soup is read, the children go on a nature walk to find some appropriate stones to begin the soup on the following day. Discuss what vegetables would be appropriate for the soup and ask each child to bring one vegetable as a contribution to the soup, as the people of the village did. Have an ample supply of vegetables on hand in case children forget to bring them in.

On the day of the cooking activity, prepare an experience chart. Begin by displaying all the vegetables that were contributed and some that you brought. Draw the following experience chart including all the vegetables and naming each one as it is drawn.

When everything has been drawn and safety rules discussed, begin by gathering the utensils needed. Boil water in a pot and put in one of the stones that has been collected. Boil the stone in the water for a few minutes to sterilize it, then remove it from the water and empty the water. Refill the pot with fresh water, add the stone and then begin cleaning the vegetables while waiting for the water to boil. Slowly add vegetables noting how they change in appearance and texture from raw to cooked. When all vegetables have been added, cover the pot and let soup simmer while the children clean up. Prepare enough soup so that, although each child in the group might not have participated in the preparation, each gets a taste. Conclude the cooking activity by re-reading *Stone Soup* and leading a discussion related to the story and cooking experience.

HOW MANY SHOULD COOK

Cooking activities are meaningful if every child who is interested in the activity actually gets to participate. Limit the size of the group that cooks on any given day to approximately six children. If you cook often enough this will not be a problem. There should also be a task for each child to do. It is not necessary that every child who begins a cooking activity remain with it until its conclusion. However, try to maintain a small enough group to be manageable. Parents and older students are excellent helpers for cooking activities and can be utilized if told far enough in advance.

The *Child's Play* recipes have been selected on the basis of their nutritious appeal and ease of preparation. Some sweet items have been included for special occasions, although they should not be exclusively used for snacks. Snacks are meant to supplement daily food needs. They give children the extra energy they need to tide them over from one meal to the next. Here are some bite size snack suggestions which are nutritious and easily prepared in the classroom.

Apple wedges	Dried peaches	Plums
Banana slices	Dried pears	Raisins
Berries	Fresh peach wedges	Prunes
Cabbage wedges	Fresh pear wedges	Melon cubes
Carrot sticks	Fresh pineapple sticks	Orange sections
Cauliflowerets	Grapefruit sections	Tangerines
Celery sticks	Green pepper sticks	Tomato wedges
Cheese cubes	Meat cubes	Turnip sticks

Breakfast and Healthy Baked Snacks

Pancakes
Put in a mixing bowl
     3/4 cup milk
     2 tablespoons melted butter
     1 egg
Beat lightly
Add
     3/4 cup flour
     2 teaspoons baking powder
     2 tablespoons sugar
     1/2 teaspoon salt
Cook in frying pan
Variation: Peanut Butter Pancakes
     Split 8 medium bananas in half
     Combine 2 cups milk
1/2 1/2 cup peanut butter
     Add 2 cups pancake mix
     Stir until fairly smooth
Makes 16 pancakes.

Carrot Bread

4 eggs well beaten
2 cups sugar
1½ cups wesson oil
3 cups flour
2 teaspoons baking soda
3 teaspoons baking powder
1/4 teaspoon salt
1 jar junior baby food carrots
4 teaspoons cinnamon
1 cup chopped nuts (optional)

Combine eggs, sugar, add oil, flour, soda, baking powder and salt. Add carrots, cinnamon and nuts. Mix well. Pour into greased 10" pan. Bake in 350º oven for about 1 hour or until cake is done. 8-12 servings.

Banana Nut Bread

Mix in a bowl:

      3 ripe bananas well masked

2   2 eggs beaten until light

2   2 tablespoons melted butter

Sift together and add to the above:

      2 cups flour

      3/4 cup sugar

      1 teaspoon salt

      1 teaspoon baking soda

Add:

      1/2 cup nuts chopped

Stir well. Put in buttered loaf pan 5" x 9". Bake 1 hour at 350°

Corn Bread

Mix and Sift together:

      3/4 cup corn meal

      1 cup flour

      1/3 cup sugar

      3 teaspoons baking powder

      3/4 teaspoon salt

Add:

      1 cup milk

      1 egg well beaten

      2 tablespoons butter well melted

Bake in a shallow buttered pan. 8" x 8" at 425° for 20 minutes.

Pumpkin Bread

3 cups sugar	1 teaspoon nutmeg
1 cup oil	1 teaspoon cinnamon
4 eggs	1 can pumpkin
1½ teaspoon salt	3½ cups flour
2 teaspoons soda	2/3 cups water

Beat eggs. Add the oil, pumpkin and sugar.

Beat well. Add sifted dry ingredients alternately with water.

Beat. Pour into 3 well greased baking pans. Bake at 350° for 60 minutes.

Peanut Butter Bread

2 cups all purpose flour   1 teaspoon salt
1/3 cup sugar   3/4 cups peanut butter
2 tsp. baking powder   1 egg well beaten
1 cup milk

Butter a 5" x 9" loaf pan. Put in the oven at 350°. Sift together the flour, sugar, baking powder and salt. Add the peanut butter and egg. Work in with a fork. Stir in milk. Spoon into pan. Bake 50 minutes or until loaf shrinks from the pan.

Granola

1/2 cup crushed almonds

1 teaspoon vanilla

1/3 cup honey

1/2 cup safflower oil

1/2 cup shredded coconut

1 cup wheat germ

1/2 cup sesame seeds

2 cups rolled oats

1/2 cup millet

1/2 cup raisins

Mix ingredients and spread on a cookie sheet. Bake at 300° for about 30 minutes. Makes 6 cups.
Note: Granola is good plain – as a dessert topping for fruit or with milk as a cereal. It is very nutritious and delicious food.

Pumpernickel Bread (a yeast bread)

In a warm bowl dissolve
    3 packages yeast in
    1½ cups lukewarm water
Stir in
    1/2 cup molasses
    3 tablespoons caraway seeds
    1 tablespoon salt
Mix together
    2 tablespoons soft butter
    3 cups sifted rye flour
Add 3 cups sifted white flour
Turn dough out onto a lightly floured board.
Knead the dough for aoubt 8-10 minutes or until smooth.
Put dough into a buttered bowl and turn it until it is cooled.
Cover the dough with a damp towel and let it rise in a warm
place until it doubles in bulk — about 2 hours.

Punch it down, divide it in half and shape each half into a ball.
Put the balls od dough on a baking sheet and sprinkle with corn
meal. Cover with a damp towel and let them rise 45 minutes.
Brush the top of the loaves with water and bake them in a 450
degree oven for 10 minutes. Reduce heat and bake in a 350°
oven for 30 minutes more — let cool.

Note: Bread is at least a 5 hour project. Great for day care or
done in 2 days with nursery.

General Snacks

Popcorn

Utensils:

    2 quart saucepan with a tight lid

    1/2 cup fresh popping corn

Place corn in pan. Cover it and move it back and forth over the burner. As corn begins to pop, keep shaking the pan rapidly until the popping stops. Remove it from the stove and empty the popped corn into a bowl.

Variations:

Popcorn Balls: Prepare a syrup of 1 cup sugar & 2 cups water. Put this in a saucepan and cook over high heat, stirring all the time with a wooden spoon. Let the mixture come to a hard boil. When ready stir the popcorn in to make caramel popcorn balls.

Chocolate Popcorn Delight

Melt 2 ounces of semi-sweet cooking chocolate in the top of a double boiler. Stir in 1/4 cup of condensed milk and keep stiring until the mixture gets thick. Remove from heat and let cool. Set over at 350°. Stir in 1½ cups of popcorn. Place by tablespoon on a greased cookie sheet pressing each mound together. Bake for 10 minutes. Remove and cool.

Jello Whip

1 package Jello

2 cups warm water

Empty a package of Jello into a bowl. Add two cups of warm water. Stir until Jello powder dissolves. Set the bowl in the refrigerator until Jello is set firmly. Take from refrigerator and beat with a rotary beater until it is light and frothy. Add a dab of whipped cream if desired and serve for snack.

Cottage Cheese

1 quart skimmed milk
1 rennet or junket tablet
3/4 teaspoon salt
1/2 cup sour cream or yogurt

Heat skimmed milk until lukewarm. Soak rennet or junket tablet in one teaspoon water. Add tablet to milk, stir well, and let stand until set. (Approximately 30 min.) Place in the top of a double boiler over low heat. Fasten cooking thermometer to edge. Stir frequently until desired temperature (110° F) for soft curd — (120° F) for farmer style.

Pour into a strainer lined with cheese cloth.
Gather corners of cloth around curds and squeeze out the whey.
Put cheese into a dish and add salt & sour cream.
Garnish with paprika. Let cheese stand 1/2 hour, before serving.

Butter

1 Pint heavy cream
1 Jar with screw top
Salt

Pour cream into jar. Pass around the circle of children allowing each of them to take a few shakes. When it begins to get thick, stop and take a look at it. It will go from whipped cream to butter. Pour off the liquid. Color or flavor if wanted. Serve on crackers or toast.

Peanut Butter

2 bags of peanuts in the shells
1/2 cup oil
pinch salt

Shell the peanuts and place in a bowl. Step up a food grinder and feed the peanuts into the grinder with a small holed attachment so that the peanuts come out in small fine chunks. Add oil and salt slowly to taste. Serve on crackers for snack.

Note: The fun of this recipe is the enjoyment the children get out of shelling their own peanuts and feeding them into the grinder. This activity has gone on all morning with a group of 3's and 4's.

Fruit and Vegetable Treats

Greenhouse Salad

Lettuce	Cucumber
Spinach	Greenbeans
Parsley	Celery
Any other greens you like.	Chive

Tear the lettuce and spinach into small pieces. Wash greenbeans.
Break them in half. Add them to the bowl. Slice the cucumber,
celery, parsley and chives. Add to mixture.
Mix well and season with salt and pepper.

Some green herbs and spices to feel, smell, taste, etc.

Mint	Spearmint	Dill
Sage	Chive	Chervil
Parsley	Tarragon	

Put greens in separate containers and describe how each one
looks. Which are the same? Which are different? Do any taste
the same? Do any have no taste?

Vegetable Soup

Cut into small pieces:

1/2 cup of	5 tablespoons butter
Carrot	1 quart water or bouillion
Celery	Salt & Pepper
Turnip	1/2 tablespoon finely cut parsley
Potato	
Peas (if available)	
Any other vegetable you wish to use.	

Wash all the vegetables. Cut celery into 1/4" slices.
Scrape carrots, peal potatoes – Dice.
Melt 4 tablespoons of butter in a large sauce pan and add all the
vegetables except potatoes. Cook 10 minutes. Add potatoes.
Cook for 2 minutes more. Add water and boil until vegetables
are soft. Add more water as needed. Season with salt and pepper.
Add the rest of the butter. Sprinkle with parsley.

Corn Chowder

1½ inch cube salt pork cut small
1 onion diced
4 potatoes cubed and sliced
3 tablespoons butter

2 cups water
2 cups creamed corn
4 cups scalded milk
Salt & Pepper

Cook the pork slowly in a deep pan until fat melts and pork bits are brown. Add onion and cook slowly 5 minutes stirring often. Remove onion and pork if you like — add potatoes and water to fat. Cook until potatoes are soft. Add corn and milk. Heat, season, add butter.

Alphabet Soup

Cook in:
    2 tablespoons butter
    1 cup cut carrots
    1/2 cup chopped onions
    1/2 cup chopped celery
    1/2 pound hamburg
    or anything else that sounds good to you!

Add:
    4 cups water
    1 can tomatoes
    alphabet noodles (as many words as you can spell)
    1 tablespoon parsley
    1 bay leaf
    1/2 teaspoon salt
    1/4 teaspoon pepper

Applesauce

    1 bag apples
    water — about 1/2 cup
    Honey
    cinnamon

Cut each apple into 4 pieces. Put the apples into a big pot. Add water. Cook them until the apples get soft. Put the applesauce through a strainer. Put the applescaue back on the stove. Add enough honey so the apples won't be sour. Sprinkle with cinnamon. Serve hot or cold.

Cranberry Sauce

1 pound cranberries
1 cup honey
2 cups water

Put the ingredients into a big pot. Mix them up. Cook until they boil quickly, stirring until the honey dissolves. Cook the berries until they pop open (about 5 minutes).

Cranberry Orange Relish

Wash:
      2 cups cranberries
      Cut into pieces and remove the seeds from 1 small orange.
      Put the fruit through a food chopper and
Add:
      3/4 cup honey
Mix thoroughly and let stand 30 minutes or more. Serves 6-8.
Have a Happy Thanksgiving!

Apple Jelly

Wash 5 or 6 tart cooking apples and cut them into pieces.
Do not remove cores or seeds.
Place in a deep saucepan and cover with water.
Cook over low heat until apples are soft and tender.

Transfer apples and liquid into a jelly bag or double piece of cheesecloth and allow to drip into a bowl.
Do not squeeze bag if you want a clear jelly.
Measure the juice and return it to the saucepan.
Add an equal amount of sugar.

Bring to a boil and continue boiling stirring constantly and testing all the time.
(The test is to pour a few drops onto a cool plate). When it jells on the plate it is done.
Remove immediately from hat and stir in a few drops of vanilla.

Pour into sterilized jelly glasses and cover with melted parafin.
Label and Date each jar.
If used right away it is not necessary to sterilize and pour parafin into jars.

Apple Crisp

4 cups pared tart apples
3/4 cup brown sugar
1/2 cup granola
1/2 cup flour
3/4 teaspoon cinnamon
3/4 teaspoon nutmeg
1/3 cup margarine

Heat oven to 375°.
Grease 8"x8"x2" pan.
Place apples in the pan.
Mix the remaining in-
gredients thoroughly.
Sprinkle over the apples.
Bake 30 minutes or un-
tile the apples are tender
and brown.

Party and Holiday Favorites

Brownies

Melt:
      2 squares unsweetened chocolate
      1 stick butter
Cool.
Add:
      1 cup sugar
      2 eggs beaten
      pinch salt
      1/2 teaspoon vanilla
      1/2 cup flour

Bake in 8" x 8" pan at 325° for 30 minutes.

Toll House Cookies

1/2 cup softened butter
1 egg
1/2 cup sugar
1/4 cup firmly packed brown sugar
1 teaspoon vanilla
1 cup flour
1/2 teaspoon baking soda
1/2 teaspoon salt
1/2 cup nuts
1 cup semisweet chocolate chips

Combine butter, egg, sugar and vanilla. Beat until light and fluffy. Beat in flour, baking soda, salt.
Stir in nuts and chips.
Drop by teaspoon on ungreased cookie sheets leaving 2" between cookies.
Bake in 375° oven for 8-10 minutes.

Peanut Butter Cookies

1/2 cup soft butter (one stick) 1/2 teaspoon salt
1/2 cup white sugar 1/2 teaspoon vanilla
1/2 cup brown sugar 1½ cups flour – sifted
1 egg 1/2 teaspoon baking soda
1 cup peanut butter

Place butter, white sugar and brown sugar in a bowl. Cream these ingredients until they are light and fluffy, like whipped cream. Beat in the egg, peanut butter, salt and vanilla. Sift the flour and baking soda and stir into the other mixture until they are blended. Roll the dough into 1" balls. Place them on a greased cookie sheet. Press them flat with a fork. Bake at 375° for about 15 minutes.

Refrigerator Lace Cookies

Stir until well blended:
> 1/2 cup white sugar 1/2 teaspoon baking soda
> 1 cup brown sugar 1/2 cup soft butter
> 1/2 cup all purpose flour 1 tablespoon milk
> 1/2 teaspoon salt 1½ teaspoon orange rind

Work in with hands or mixer 1 cup rolled oats. Preheat oven to 350°. Drop cookie dough onto greased cookie sheet. Bake 8-10 minutes. Note: Can also mix dough and form into 2" diameter balls. Place in foil – wrap securely and place in a refrigerator 12-24 hours. Then remove, slice thinly and bake.

Gingerbread Men

Mix in bowl:
> 2/3 cup butter 1 teaspoon soda dissolved in
> 1½ cupsugar 3 tablespoons sour milk
> 2 eggs (Make the milk sour by putting
> 3-4 cups flour 1 tablespoon vinegar in 1 cup milk.)
> 1 teaspoon cinnamon Divide into 15 balls and chill the
> 1 teaspoon cloves dough.
> 1/2 teaspoon ginger
> 1/4 teaspoon salt

Press the dough into gingerbread man shape being careful to overlap the head, arms and legs to body. Decorate with raisens. Bake about 10 minutes at 375°. Yield 15 gingerbread men. Note: Dough may be rolled and cut with cookie cutters. This is a marvelous Christmas Tree ornament.

NOTE: Important!

Please, please take extra precaution when working with candy. The temperature of the liquid gets extremely hot and can cause bad burns. An adult MUST be present AT ALL TIMES and for no minute should leave the activity unsupervised. Save this activity for a time when you are sure the rest of your group is busy and cared for. Select your children carefully and explain the procedure well beforehand emphasizing the directions.

Lillipops

In a two quart sauce pan stir:
> 1/2 teaspoon vanilla
> 2 cups sugar
> 3/4 cup corn syrup
> 1 cup water

Place over low flame and stir until all the sugar is melted. Then place cover on pot and allow to come to full boil. Remove cover and place candy thermometer in. Allow to cook over high flame without further stirring until thermometer reads 300°. Remove from flame and add sufficient color to tint candy well. Stir in vanilla. Pour hot liquid very carefully onto aluminum foil (shiney side) by the tablespoon full. Press a popsicle stick into each Lollipop. Remove from foil when cold.

Variation: Candy Apples

Use the lollipop recipe and make coating only color you want. Select perfect ripe red apples and wash them well. Dry carefully before dipping. Press lollipop stick into fruit at the stem indentation. Be sure apple is firmly mounted.

As soon as candy coating has been cooked to the proper temperature, holding the pan tilted to keep candy deep, rotate an apple slowly in the syrup until completely covered. Immediately stand the apple upright on a piece of waxed paper. Allow to harden

Custard Ice Cream

Scald:

    1½ cups milk

Mix until smooth:

    1 tablespoon corn starch or flour

    3/4 cup sugar

    1/4 cup cold milk

Add:

    the scalded milk slowly and cook stirring over hot water 8 minutes.

Add:

    1 egg or 2 egg yolks slightly beaten

Cook 2 minutes — Cool

Add:

    1 pint cream

    1 tablespoon vanilla

    1/4 teaspoon salt

Procedure:

1. Prepare the Ice Cream Mix.
2. Prepare ice by placing chunks or cubes of ice in a bag and breaking into smaller pieces with a flat edged hammer.
3. Insert dasher in can. Be sure the protrusion in the bottom of the dasher fits into the socket of the freezer can.
4. Pour mix into freezer can. Do not fill more than 2/3 full. Put on the can cover. Check to see if the dasher moves freely.
5. Assemble the can in the tub. Be sure the can rests in the proper position on the stud in the bottom of the tub.
6. Place gear frame in position.
7. Add the ice to about 3" deep in the bottom of tub. Sprinkle around approximately 1/3 cup of Rock Salt then alternate the ice and salt until the level of the ice and salt is on the top of the freezer can. Avoid getting the salt on the top of the freezer can so the salt will not seep in.
8. Turn dasher slowly for the first 2 or 3 minutes to allow mix to cool. When it appears to freeze, turn dasher more rapidly to beat some air in.
9. Discontinue churning when handle becomes extremely difficult to turn.
10. Remove dasher and scrape the extra ice cream back in the can. Place can in freezer for about 30 minutes.

Taken From: From with Food
          New England Dairy and Food Council
          August, 1971

Variations:
1. Chocolate — make custard ice cream melting 2 squares chocolate with milk as it is scalded. Increase suguar to 1¼ cups.
2. Coffee Ice Cream — Favor to taste with instant coffee and brandy.
3. Strawberry — Mash 1 quart berries. Sprinkle with 1/2 cup sugar. Let stand 20 minutes. Strain if desired.

NOTE:

The recipes for ice cream and the toppings can be prepared on four consecutive days and stored in the refrigerator.

On the fifth day all are served to the children as an ice cream smorgasbord party where they could choose their own topping.

This week of cooking was the culmination of the trip to the dairy farm and concided with the last week of school. Actually, it can be done anytime and for any occasion.

Chocolate Sauce

Melt in a double boiler:
    5 oz. unsweetened chocolate (5-1oz. squares)
    1/2 cup butter (1 stick)
Remove from heat.
Add:
    3 cups of unsifted confestioners sugar
Alternate with:
    1 large can evaporated milk
Bring to a boil. Cook until the sauce is thick and creamy.
Stir constantly. Remove from heat.
Add:
    2 teaspoons vanilla

Marshmallow Sauce

Place in small bowl:
    1 cup Marshmallow fluff
Add:
    Water in small amounts and blend with a fork to desired consistency.
Can be stored in plastic capped container in the refrigerator.

Butterscotch Sauce

Mix in a double boiler:

> 1/2 cup brown sugar
>
> 1/2 cup light corn syrup
>
> 1/4 cup light cream

Cook 20 minutes over hot water until thickened.

Add:

> 1/8 teaspoon salt
>
> 2 tablespoons butter
>
> 1 teaspoon vanilla

Stir well:

> (Can be stored in plastic capped container in the refrigerator.)

Lightning Birthday Cake

1 cup all purpose flour	1/2 cup milk
1 teaspoon baking powder	2 eggs
1/4 teaspoon salt	1 teaspoon vanilla
1 tablespoon butter	1 cup sugar

Set oven at 375°. Prepare the cake pan — 8" x 8".

Sift flour with baking powder and salt onto a piece of waxed paper. Heat milk and add the butter to it.

Beat the eggs with a beater until thick. Add the vanilla.

Add sugar a little at a time and beat until mixture is thick and fluffy. Stir in the flour mixture. Add hot milk and stir just enough to blend.

Spoon onto cake pan.

Bake about 25 minutes until the cake shrinks from the edge.

Frost.

Pink Frosting

1 box confestioner's sugar

2 teaspoons vanilla

1/2 cup soft butter

cream or milk

food color

Beat sugar, vanilla and butter together adding enough milk or cream to make frosting of spreading consistency. Add food color in amounts dependent upon your visual tastes.

Gold Cupcakes

Sift:
>   1¼ cups cake flour
>   3/4 cup sugar
>   1-3/4 teaspoon baking powder
>   1/2 teaspoon salt

Add:
>   1/4 cup butter
>   2/3 cup milk
>   1 teaspoon vanilla

Beat for 2 minutes.
Add:
>   3 egg yolks

Beat for 1 minute.
Bake in cupcake pan. Fill each cup 1/2 full.
Bake for 20 minutes at 375°.

Chocolate Kisses

1½ cups flour	½ cup soft margarine
1½ teaspoons baking powder	½ cup sugar
½ cup cocoa	1 egg

Set oven at 325°. Place all ingredients in a bowl. Mix well with spoon. Use your hands to get the mixture in one big ball. Grease the baking sheet(s). Put one teaspoon of the mixture onto the sheet using your finger to push it off the spoon. Continue until you have 15 on each of two trays — spaced well apart. Bake in the middle of the oven for 25 minutes. When they are cool — stick them together in pairs with the frosting recipe on the next page.

Chocolate Frosting

Beat until smooth:
>   1 box confestioner's sugar
>   4 squares melted unsweetened chocolate
>   1/4 cup hot water
>   1 teaspoon vanilla
>   1 egg
>   1/2 stick butter

Green Pretzels

Dissolve 1 package yeast in 1½ cups warm water.
Add:

     4 cups flour

     1 teaspoon salt

     1 tablespoon sugar

     green food coloring

Knead until smooth.

Cut into small pieces.

Roll into rope.

Shape and place on a greased cookie sheet.

Brush with a beaten egg and sprinkle with salt. Bake at 425° for 12-15 minutes or until brown.

Selected References

Callahan, Dorothy, Payne, Alma. *Young America's Cookbook.* Charles
        Scribner and Son — New York, 1959.

Cavin, Ruth, *1 Pinch of Sunshine, ½ Cup of Rain.* Atheneum. N. Y., 1973.

Davis, Barbara, *Learning Science Through Cooking.* Sterling Publishing Co.
        New York. 1960.

DeGros, J. H., *Holiday Candy and Cookie Cookbook.* Arco Publishing Co.
        New York. 1964.

Fisher, Kathleen Dunning. *Cook-In.* David White Co. New York. 1969.

Freeman, Mae Blacker. *Fun with Cooking.* Random House. 1947.

Fun with Food. A Teachers Supplement for Nutrition Education Projects
        for Kindergarten Children. New England Dairy Council, Mass. 1971.

Glovich, Linda. *The Little Witch's Black Magic Cookbook.* Prentice Hall
Inc   Inc. New Jersey. 1972.

Hautzigie. *Cool Cooking, 16 Recipes without a Stove.* Lothrop, Lee &
        Shephard. New York. 1973

Perkins, Wilma Lord. *The Fanny Farmer Junior Cookbook.* Little Brown
        and Co. Boston, Mass. 1957.

Perret Denise, Eckley, Mary. *The Young French Chef.* Platta and Munk,
        New York, 1955.

Children's Story Books on Cooking

Anderson, Carolyn. *Complete Book of Homemade Ice Cream.* Saturday Re-
        view Press. N. Y. 1972.

Goldin, Augusta. *Where Does Your Garden Grow?* Crowell Co. N.Y. 1967.

Greenaway, Kate. *A. Apple Pie.* Frederick Warne and Co. London. 1886.

Hoban, Russell, *Bread & Jam for Frances.*

Janice, *Little Bear's Pancake Party.* Lothrop. New York. 1969.

Janice, *Little Bear's Thanksgiving.* Lothrop. New York. 1960.

Kahl, Virginia. *The Dutchess Bakes a Cake.* Scribner. 1955.

Lindquist, Willia. *Stone Soup.* Western Publishing Co. 1970.

Mannheim, Grere. *The Baker's Children. a visit to a Family Bakery.* Al-
        fred Knopf, N.Y. 1970.

Montresor, Beni. *May I Bring a Friend?* Atheneum. New York. 1971.

Moore, Eva. *The Cookie Book.* Seabury Press. N. Y. 1973.

Selsam, Millicent. *More Potatoes!* Harper and Row. New York. 1972.

Selsam, Millicent. *Vegetables from Stems and Leaves.* William Morrow.
        N. Y. 1972.

Sendak, Maurice. *Chicken Soup with Rice.* Harper and Row. New York.
        1962.

Russell, S. P. Peanuts, Popcorn. Ice Cream. Candy, Soda Pop. Abington
        Press, N.Y. 1970.

appendix

These developmental guidelines are included as a checklist of charactistic behaviors oc children aged two to six. Items listed in the guidelines are grouped into areas of child development which include:

Motor Development
Social Development
Intellectual Development

There are variations in the appearance of developmental charactistics in all children, some appearing earlier or later than charted. These developmental guidelines represent selected charactistics of the majority of normal healthy children between the ages of two and w six.

TWO YEARS

MOTOR DEVELOPMENT

1. **Gross**
   a. has reached the stage of independent walking having gone through the stages of sitting, crawling, standing and walking
   b. walks up and down stairs without assistance
   c. moves into large running more confidently
   d. more aware of individual body parts
   e. leaps down with one foot leading

2. **Fine**
   a. grasps things with more assureness
   b. likes to tinker with small things like cars and small toys
   c. scribbles
   d. manipulates objects

SOCIAL, EMOTIONAL

1. **Language**
   a. associates symbols (words) to objects and uses words meaningfully
   b. comprehends questions
   c. vocabulary increases rapidly
   d. begins to be aware of grammar — predominance of nouns
   e. imitates extensively
   f. interested in stories and records

guidelines for developmental skills
characteristics of preschool children

THREE YEARS

MOTOR DEVELOPMENT

1. **Gross**
   a. runs with more smoothness
   b. turns sharp corners, negotiates sudden stops
   c. alternates feet going up and down stairs
   d. jumps with both feet together
   e. can stand on one foot for a few seconds
   f. dresses and undresses himself

2. **Fine**
   a. can fold paper horizontally
   b. likes to manipulate clay, small blocks and shapes
   c. begins to show a hand preference — can better control crayons and pencils

SOCIAL, EMOTIONAL

1. **Language**
   a. adds many new words to vocabulary
   b. speaks more in sentences — sentences are longer
   c. uses language more efficiently and flexibly
   d. better mastery of grammar
   e. talks constantly
   f. imitates more
   g. communication allows him to see more connection between things

characteristics of preschool children
guidelines for developmental skills

TWO YEARS

**SOCIAL,
EMOTIONAL**

2. Play

a. imitates play

b. intensively curious about his surroundings

c. moves about freely

d. explores vigorously

e. developing a sense of autonomy and competence ,mpe-

f. learns about the ability to make choices

g. discovers his own physical limits

h. plays alone

3. Relationship

a. wants love and guidance

b. needs to feel useful

c. out for himself — selfish and possessive

d. goes about individual activities with other children side by side

e. easier to deal with through distraction rather than reasoning

f. relationships tend to be short

g. spends time watching others play

h. anxious in new situations involving loss of interest in them

4. Toilet Training

a. might tend to be a source of friction because the mothers role is changing from a feeder, care taker to someone who expects child to assume more independence and responsibility for his own care.

characteristics of preschool children
guidelines for developmental skills

THREE YEARS

SOCIAL,
EMOTIONAL

2. Play
    a. does not share well but is trying to learn
    b. really into parallel play (side by side) also solitary play
    c. much more into imitation of parental roles in dramatic play
    d. enjoys dressing up in costumes
    e. beginning to show self control over emotions

3. Relationship
    a. much more interested in other children
    b. still tends to be selfish
    c. tries to please adults
    d. feels sympathetic towards other children
    e. feels proud of what he does
    f. developing more feelings of independence
    g. naps during the day
    h. learning how to take turns
    i. able to leave mother for a long enough time to come to school

4. Toilet Training
    a. trained for the most part but still may have some accidents. Not very anxious about these for the most part.

characteristics of preschool children
guidelines for developmental skills

TWO YEARS

INTELLECTUAL DEVELOPMENT

a. interested in stories and records

b. associates more emphatically

c. becomes more objective

d. tasks are more goal oriented

e. more actively experiments with materials

f. cognitive functions more oriented toward reality

g. names pictures — identifies objects

h. can do some counting and letter naming

i. can identify major body parts

PHYSICAL DEVELOPMENT

a. slower than first year

b. grows about 4" — gains about 4-5 lbs.

c. fatter children are slightly taller than lean ones.

d. bones increase in size — become more calcified

e. body more in proportion

f. brain becomes heavier

g. nervous system is more complex

characteristics of preschool children
guidelines for developmental skills

THREE YEARS

INTELLECTUAL DEVELOPMENT

a. reacts to entire stimulus rather than individual parts
b. likes to talk with adults
c. listens to longer stories
d. can appreciate simple humor
e. can point out three items in a picture

PHYSICAL DEVELOPMENT

a. boy about 38" — 33 lbs.
   girl about 37" — 32 lbs.
b. upper body parts begin to approximate adult size
c. limb growth is rapid
d. becomes more fussy about foods
e. body more in proportion
f. brain becomes heavier
g. nervous system more complex

FOUR YEARS

**SOCIAL,
EMOTIONAL
(Continued)**

f. very inquisitive about the how and why of things

g. begins to develop imagination and imaginary playmates

h. play becomes more associative — will talk with others in block corner or doll corner — plans activities with them

i. will switch allegiances with friends easily and quickly

j. acts very silly if tired

k. developing a real sense of autonomy

**INTELLECTUAL
DEVELOPMENT**

a. points out more detailed things in pictures

b. can follow directions

c. has a much longer attention span

d. recalls information told to him

e. learns to classify and categorize information and objects can put things in proper sequence

f. very interested in what other people's families are like — makes comparisons with his family

g. developing discrimination in the senses

h. more developed auditory and visual discrimination and can now see and hear differences in rhyming words, sounds, people, etc.

characteristics of preschool children
guidelines for developmental skills

FIVE YEARS

SOCIAL,
EMOTIONAL
(Continued)

d. tends to develop stronger friendships and stick with them — will defend friends if they are in trouble

e. likes humor a lot and will begin to share in it with adults using nonsense language they make up

f. likes to sing very much and enjoys all kinds of songs — quite good at remembering the words

g. enjoys the security of routines during the day

h. will act silly if tired — can get very irritable

i. gets along well with small groups of children

INTELLECTUAL
DEVELOPMENT

a. knows alphabet and numerals

b. able to do intricate puzzles

c. has an active curiosity about babies and is increasingly aware of sexual differences

d. is ready to put letters together to form simple words — recognizes that letters have sound which form words

e. developing concepts through conversation, stories, pictures, songs, dramatic play and special projects

f. is able to express ideas clearly and dictate stories

g. is able to follow through on projects that take more one day

h. can read simple maps and charts and make their own

i. begins solving problems

characteristics of preschool children
guidelines for developmental skills

FOUR YEARS

**MOTOR
DEVELOPMENT**

1. Gross
a. climbs much more actively
b. has more motor control and coordination
c. can catch a ball and throw it back over hand
d. actively runs, jumps, hops
e. can do a one legged skip
f. can do a running broad jump
g. can saw a straight line

2. Fine
a. can begin to print name
b. begins to have control in using scissors
c. artwork has more form — more easily recognizable objects and sense of design and color
d. can manipulate puzzle pieces and small game pieces with ease

**SOCIAL,
EMOTIONAL**
a. continuing sensitivity towards people
b. learning to share materials and ideas — also learning to compromise
c. is learning and testing limits
d. is anxious to tell children and adults about new adventures
e. still finds it difficult to recognize teacher

characteristics of preschool children
guidelines for developmental skills

FIVE YEARS

MOTOR DEVELOPMENT

1. Gross

a. good sense of balance — learning to ride a two wheel bike

b. has more hand/eye control

c. can skip

d. jumps very smoothly

e. can walk backward on a balance beam

f. learns to tie shoes

g. can drop pellets into a bottle one at a time

2. Fine

a. can print his own name as well as the whole alphabet — is able to control smaller crayons, pencils and paint brushes

b. shows definite hand preference

d. some will draw easy to recognize pictures

d. can copy a square, triangle, and sometimes a circle — makes more detailed drawings of people

SOCIAL, EMOTIONAL

a. poised and controlled in a group of people — some are still shy and tend to stay with mother — others are extremely aggressive and outgoing

b. play is more with a group than alone — cooperative play

c. attention span is much longer — is able to develop an idea into an extensive story of his own and act it out with a group of children

Selected References

Child Development

Erikson, Erik. *Childhood and Society.* New York: Norton Publishing Co., 1963.

Gardner, Bruce. *Development in Early Childhood: The Preschool Years.* New York: Harper and Row, 1964.

Gesell, Arnold; Llg, Frances; Ames, Louise Bates; and Rodell, Janet Learned. *Infant and Child in the Culture of Today.* New York: Harper and Row, revised edition, 1974.

Mussen, P.; Conger, J.; and Kagen, J. *Child Development and Personality.* New York: Harper and Row, 1969.

Stone, L. J. Church, J. *Childhood and Adolescence: A Psychology of the Growing Person.* (3rd Edition). New York: Random House, 1973.

Wadsworth, Barry J. *Piaget's Theory of Cognitive Development.* New York: David McKay Co., Inc., 1974.

Early Childhood Education

Ashton-Warner, Sylvia. *Teacher.* New York: Simon and Schuster, 1963. Biber, Barbara; Shapiro, Edna; Wickens, David; and Gilkeson, Elizabeth. *Promoting Cognitive Growth:* A Developmental Interaction Point of View. Washington, D.C.: National Association for the Education of Young Children, 1971.

Bruner, Jerome. *The Process of Education.* Cambridge, Mass.: Harvard University Press, 1960.

Cohen, Dorothy H. *The Learning Child: Guidelines for Parents and Teachers.* New York: Pantheon Books, 1972.

Cohen, Dorothy H., Rudolph, Marguerita. *Kindergarten, A Year of Learning.* New York: Meridith Corporation, 1964.

Cohen, Dorothy H., Stern, Virginia. *Observing and Recording the Behavior of Young Children.* New York: Columbia University, 1958.

Croft, Doreen J., Hess, Robert D. *An Activities Handbook for Teachers of Young Children.* 2nd Edition. Boston: Houghton-Mifflin, 1975.

Hartley, Ruth; Frank, Lawrence; and Goldenson, R. M., *Understanding Children's Play.* New York: Crowell, 1957.

Heffernan, H., Todd, V.E. *The Years Before School.* New York: The Macmillan Co., 1964.

Hymes, J. L. *The Child Under Six.* Englewood Cliffs, N.J.: Prentice Hall, 1963.

McMurrain, T. Thomas, Brook, Fan, *Child Development Assessment Form Ages Three to Six.* Atlanta: Humanics Associates, 1975.

Read, Katherine. *The Nursery School.* 5th Edition. Philadelphia, Pa.,
W. B. Saunders, 1971.

Pitcher, E.G., and Ames, L.B. *The Guidance Nursery School.* New York:
Harper and Row, 1964.

Taylor, Barbara J. *A Child Goes Forth.* Salt Lake City: Brigham Young
University Press, 1970.

Wann, Kenneth; Dorn, M.E.; and Liddle, E.A. *Fostering Intellectual
Development in Young Children.* New York: Teachers College,
Columbia University, 1962.

Weikart, David; Rogers, Linda; and Adcock, Carolyn. *The Cognitively
Oriented Curriculum.* Washington, D.C.: National Association
for the Education of Young Children, 1974.

The Successful Teacher's Most Valuable Resource!

HUMANICS LEARNING

EDUCATION

THE EARLI PROGRAM
Excellent language development program! Volume I contains developmentally sequenced lessons in verbal receptive language; Volume II, expressive language. Use as a primary, supplemental or rehabilitative language program.

| Volume I | HL-067-7 | $14.95 |
| Volume II | HL-074-X | $14.95 |

LEARNING ENVIRONMENTS FOR CHILDREN
A practical manual for creating efficient, pleasant and stressfree learning environments for children centers. Make the best possible use of your center's space!

HL-065-0 $12.95

COMPETENCIES:
A Self-Study Guide to Teaching Competencies in Early Childhood Education
This comprehensive guide is ideal for evaluating or improving your competency in early childhood education or preparing for the CDA credential.

HL-024-3 $14.95

ENERGY:
A Curriculum for 3, 4 and 5 Year Olds
Help preschool children become aware of what energy is, the sources of energy, the uses of energy and wise energy use with the fun-filled activities, songs and games included in this innovative manual.

HL-069-3 $ 9.95

YOUNG CHILDREN'S BEHAVIOR:
Implementing Your Goals
A variety of up-to-date approaches to discipline and guidance to help you deal more effectively with children. Also an excellent addition to CDA and competency-based training programs.

HL-015-4 $ 8.95

FINGERPLAYS & RHYMES
Delight children 2-8 while teaching them about numbers, colors, shapes, holidays, self-concept, feelings, and much more. More than 250 original rhymes and fingerplays.

HL-083-9 $14.95

STORYBOOK CLASSROOMS:
Using Children's Literature in the Learning Center/Primary Grades
A guide to making effective use of children's literature in the classroom. Activities designed for independent use by children K – 3, supplemented with illustrations and patterns for easy use. Guidelines, suggestions, and bibliographies will delight and help to instill a love of reading in kids!

HL-043-X $16.95

ACTIVITY BOOKS

EARLY CHILDHOOD ACTIVITIES:
A Treasury of Ideas from Worldwide Sources
A virtual encyclopedia of projects, games and activities for children aged 3 – 7, containing over 500 different child-tested activities drawn from a variety of teaching systems. The ultimate activity book!

HL-066-9 $16.95

VANILLA MANILA FOLDER GAMES
Make exciting and stimulating **Vanilla Manila Folder Games** quickly and easily with simple manila file folders and colored marking pens. Unique learning activities designed for children aged 3 – 8.

HL-059-6 $16.95

LEAVES ARE FALLING IN RAINBOWS
Science Activities for Early Childhood
Hundreds of science activities help your children learn concepts an properties of water, air, plants, light, shadows, magnets, sound and elec tricity. Build on interests when providing science experience and they'll **always** be eager to learn!

HL-045-6 $16.95

HANDBOOK OF LEARNING ACTIVITIES
Over 125 exciting, enjoyable activities and projects for young children in the areas of math, health and safety, play, movement, science, social studies, art, language development, puppetry and more!

HL-058-8 $16.95

MONTH BY MONTH ACTIVITY GUIDE FOR THE PRIMARY GRADES
Month by Month gives you a succinct guide to the effective recruitment and utilization of teachers' aides plus a **full year's worth** of fun-filled education activities in such areas as reading, math, art, and science.

HL-061-8 $16.95

ART PROJECTS FOR YOUNG CHILDREN
Build a basic art program of stimulating projects on a limited budget and time schedule with **Art Projects**. Contains over 100 fun-filled projects in the areas of drawing, painting, puppets, clay, printing and more!

HL-051-0 $16.95

BLOOMIN' BULLETIN BOARDS
Stimulate active student participation and learning as you promote your kids' creativity with these delightful and entertaining activities in the areas of Art, Language Arts, Mathematics, Health, Science, Social Studies, and the Holidays. Watch learning skills and self-concepts blossom!

HL-047-2 $14.95

AEROSPACE PROJECTS FOR YOUNG CHILDREN
Introduce children to the fascinating field of aerospace with the exciting and informative projects and field trip suggestions. Contributors include over 30 aviation/aerospace agencies and personnel.

HL-052-9 $14.95

CHILD'S PLAY:
An Activities and Materials Handbook
An eclectic selection of fun-filled activities for preschool children designed to lend excitement to the learning process. Activities include puppets, mobiles, poetry, songs and more.

HL-003-0 $14.95

READING RESOURCE BOOK
This excellent, highly readable text gives you an overview of children's language development, suggestions for games that enhance reading skills, ideas for establishing a reading environment in the home, tips for grandparents, and lists of resources.

HL-044-8 $16.95

Humanics Publications

CHILDREN AROUND THE WORLD
Introduce preschool and kindergarten children to people and ways of other cultures.
HL-033-2 $16.95

THE FLANNELBOARD STORYBOOK
Step-by-step directions, story-telling techniques and how to make flannelboards and materials.
HL-093-6 $16.95

BIRTHDAYS: A CELEBRATION
More than 30 party themes and 200 games and activites are adaptable for children ages 3–10.
HL-075-8 $14.95

TEDDY BEARS AT SCHOOL
Learning center activities centered around teddy bears includes math, fine and gross motor skills, self concept and more. Ages 4–7
HL-092-8 $16.95

THE LOLLIPOP TEST
A Diagnostic Screening Test of School Readiness
Based on the latest research in school readiness, this test effectively measures children's readiness strengths and weaknesses. Included is all you need to give, score and interpret the test.
HL-028-6   (Specimen Set) $29.95

CAN PIAGET COOK?
Forty-six lesson plans with reproducible worksheets. Children experience science first hand with these food-related activities.
HL-078-2 $12.95

SCISSOR SORCERY
Over 50 reproducible, developmentally sequenced activity sheets help children learn to cut proficiently.
HL-076-6 $16.95

THE INFANT & TODDLER HANDBOOK
Activities for children birth to 24 months. For teachers, day care personnel, parents & other care givers.
HL-038-3 $12.95

TODDLERS LEARN BY DOING
Hundreds of activities are developmentally designed just for toddlers.
HL-085-5 $12.95

NUTS AND BOLTS
Guidelines for setting up an early learning center, organization and management.
HL-063-4 $ 8.95

THE CHILD CARE INVENTORY & MANUAL
Developed for infant & preschool programs. The Inventory reviews 11 performance areas. The manual explains how to collect, score and interpret the data.
HL-090-1   (Set) $19.95

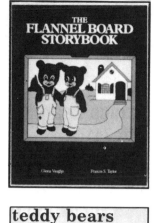

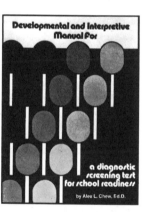

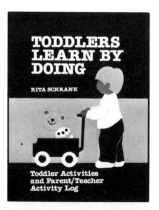

HUMANICS LEARNING

ORDER FORM

Try your local book store or school supply store for Humanics Publications.

Name _____

Address _____

City _____ State _____ Zip _____

TITLE	CODE	PRICE	QUANTITY	TOTAL

All orders from individuals must include prepayment, or credit card number and signature must be provided below.

☐ MasterCard   ☐ Visa

_____
Account Number

_____
Signature

_____
MasterCard Interbank No.   Expiration Date

_____
Institutional Purchase Order

SUBTOTAL	
Ga. Residents, add 5% sales tax	
Discount, if applicable	
Shipping and Handling	
TOTAL	

Add 15% shipping and handling

☎ ORDER TOLL FREE
1-800-874-8844
IN GA (404) 874-2176

- **Same Day Telephone Service —**
  Order toll free and we will ship your order within 48 hours.
- **Order By Phone —**
  with Visa or MasterCard

Please call for discounts and terms.